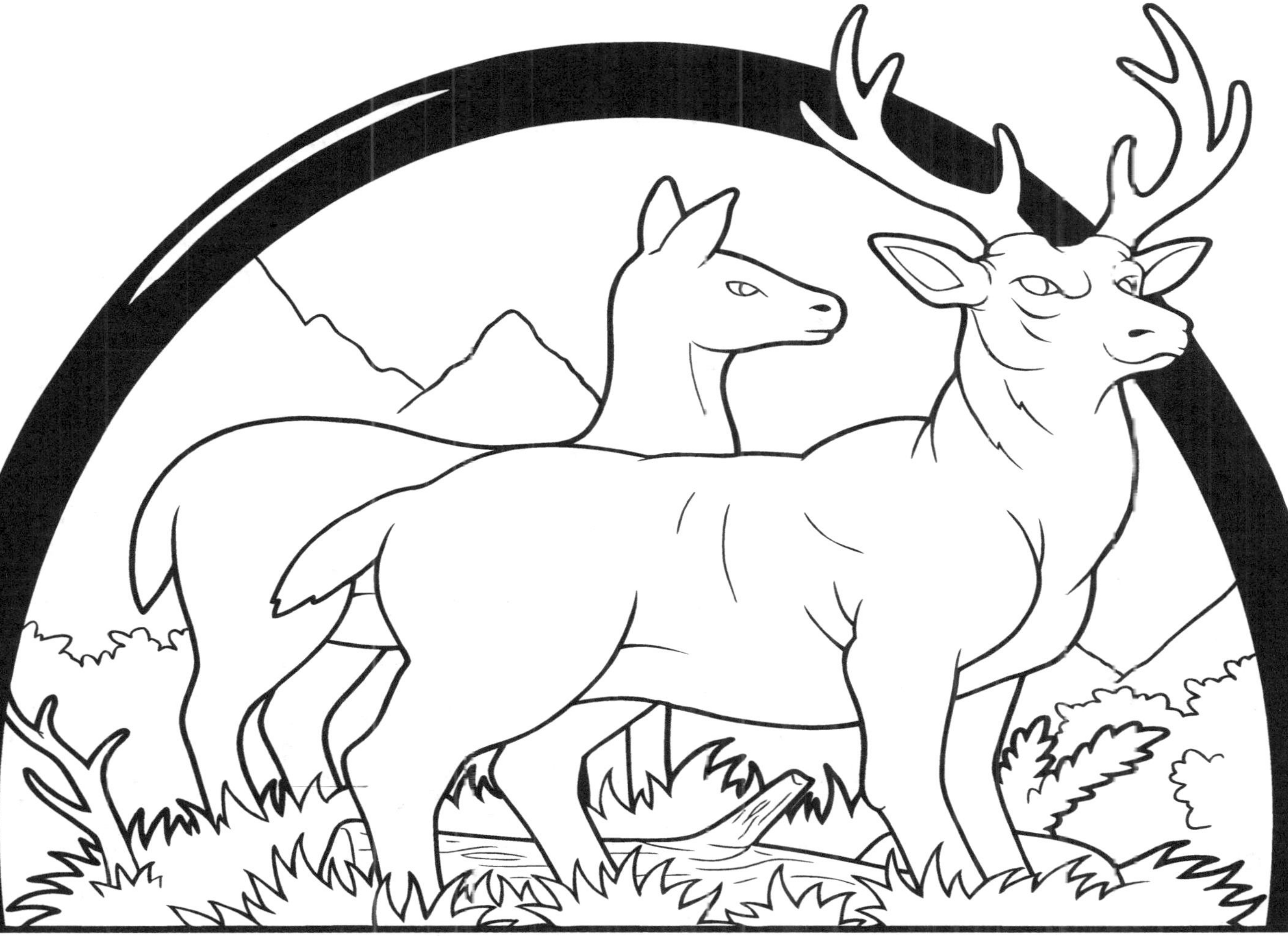

This book belongs to:

Color With Me!

Daddy & Me Coloring Book Wildlife

Mary Lou Brown
Sandy Mahony

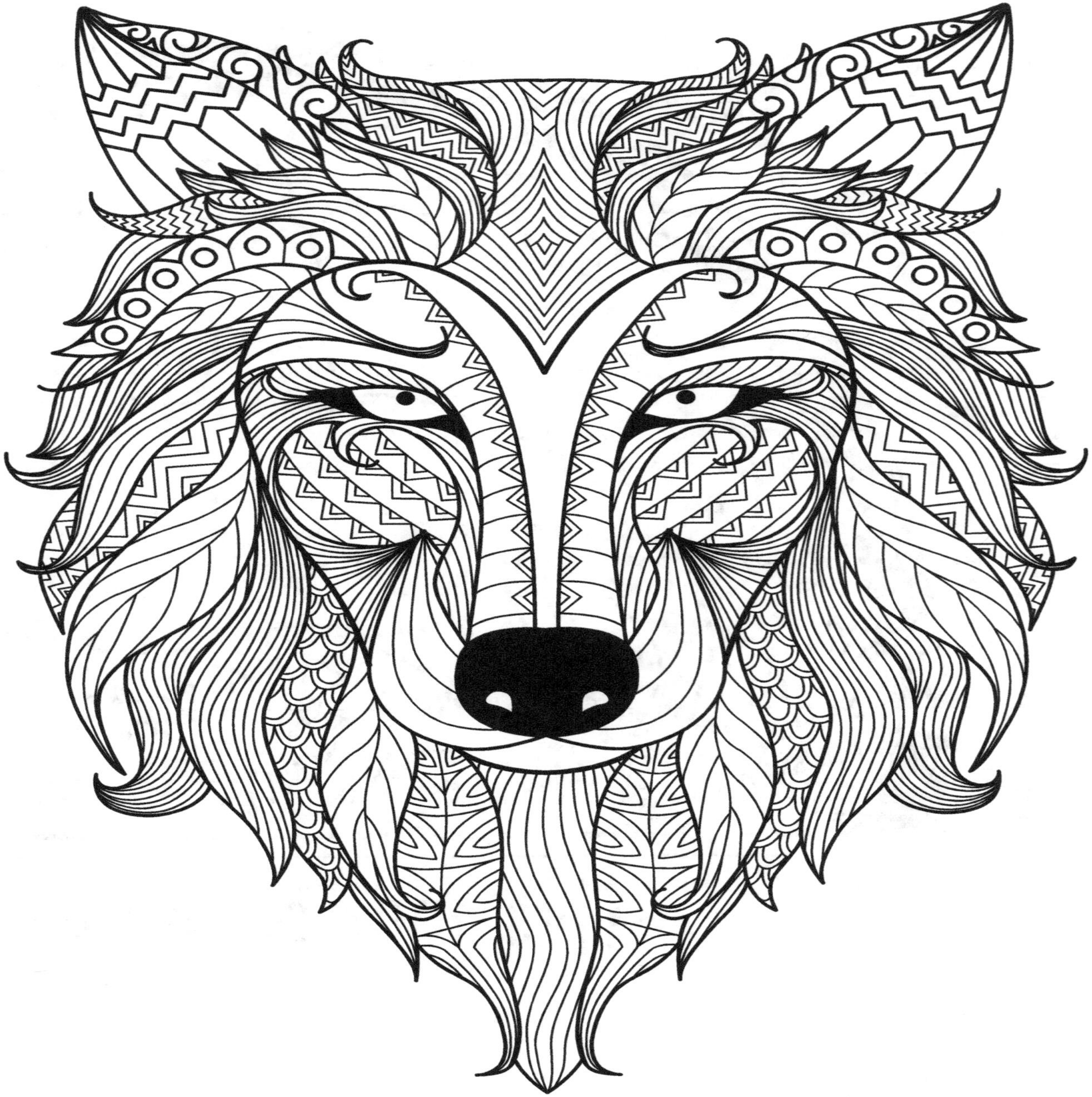

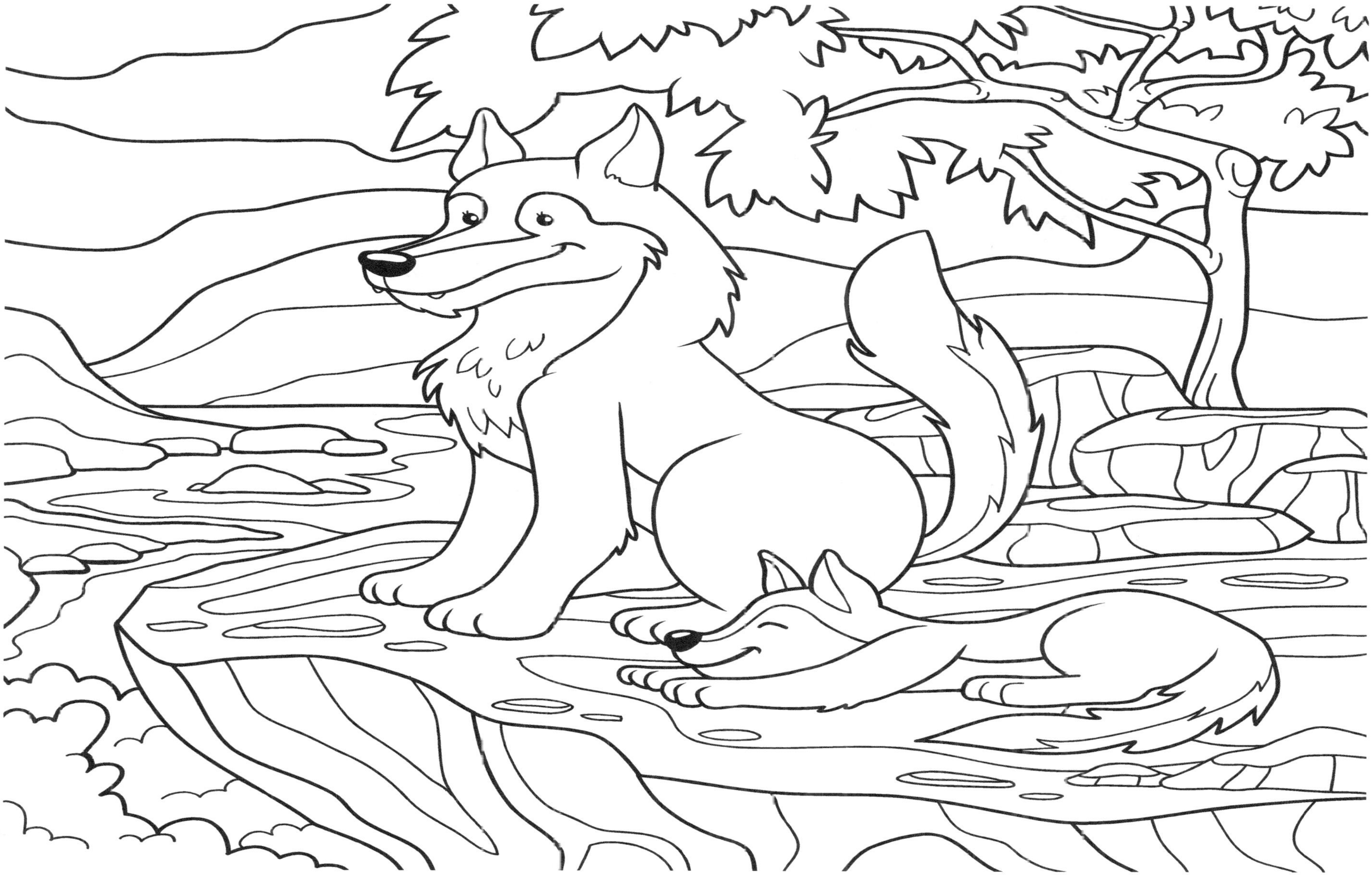

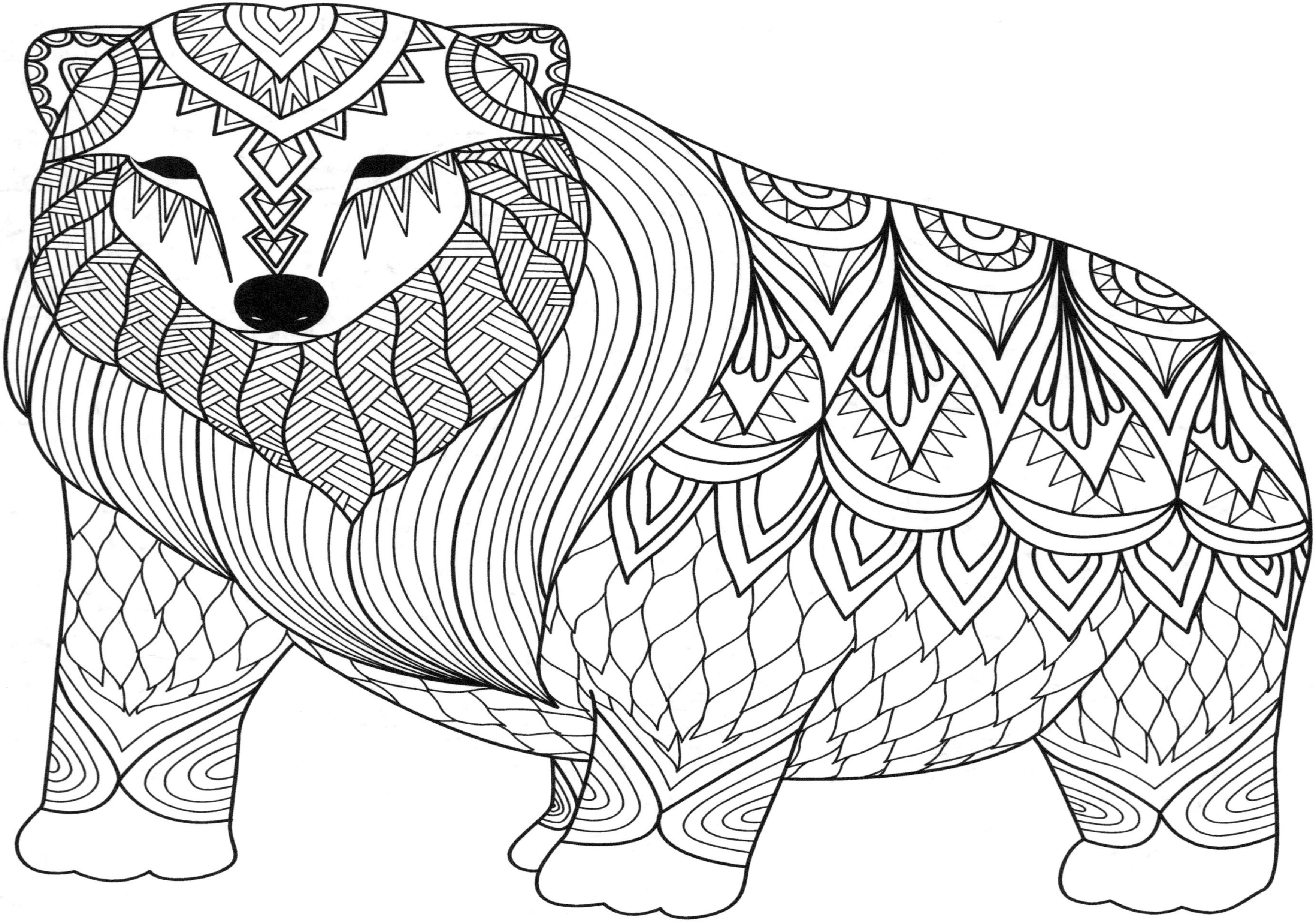

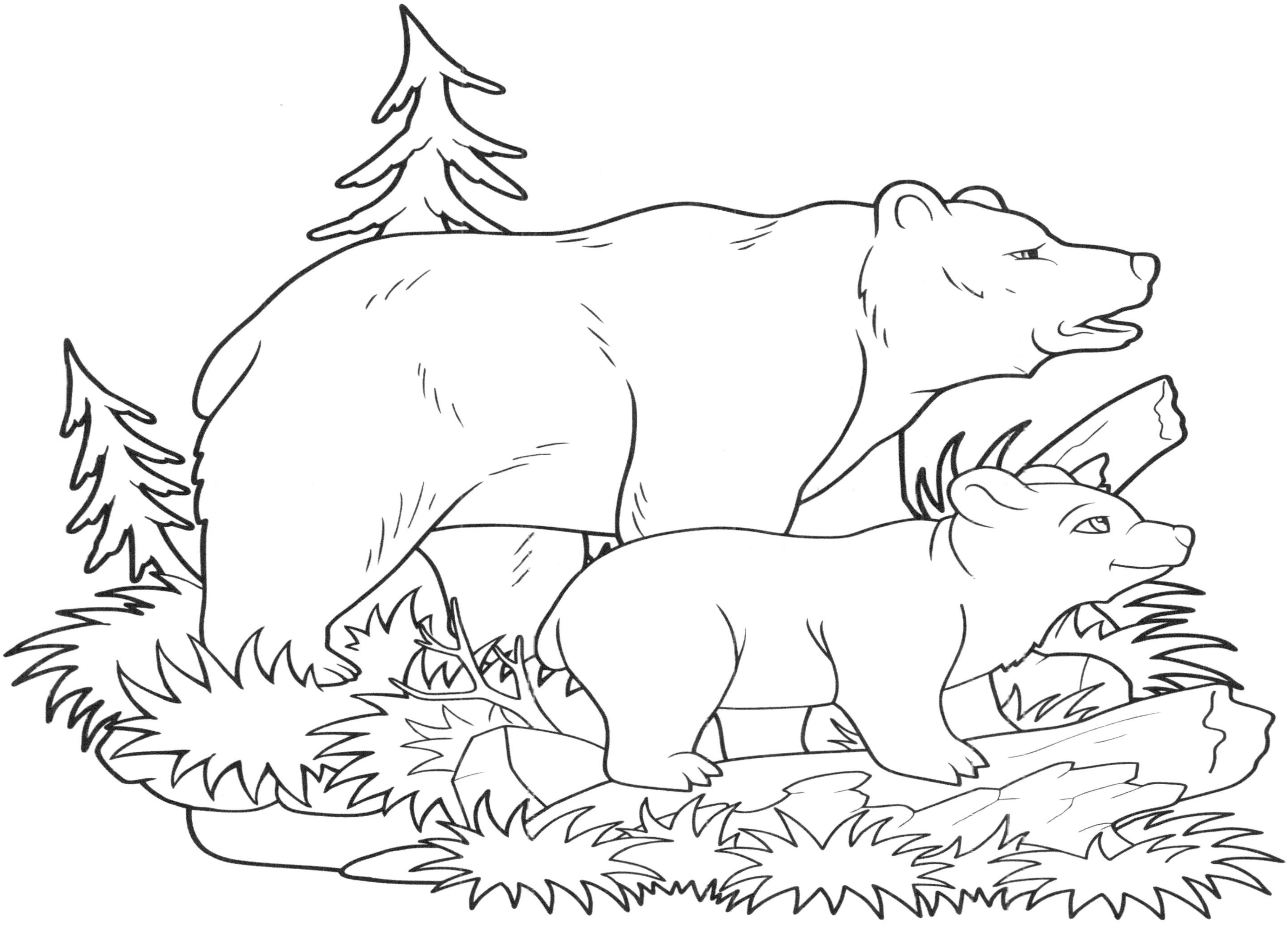

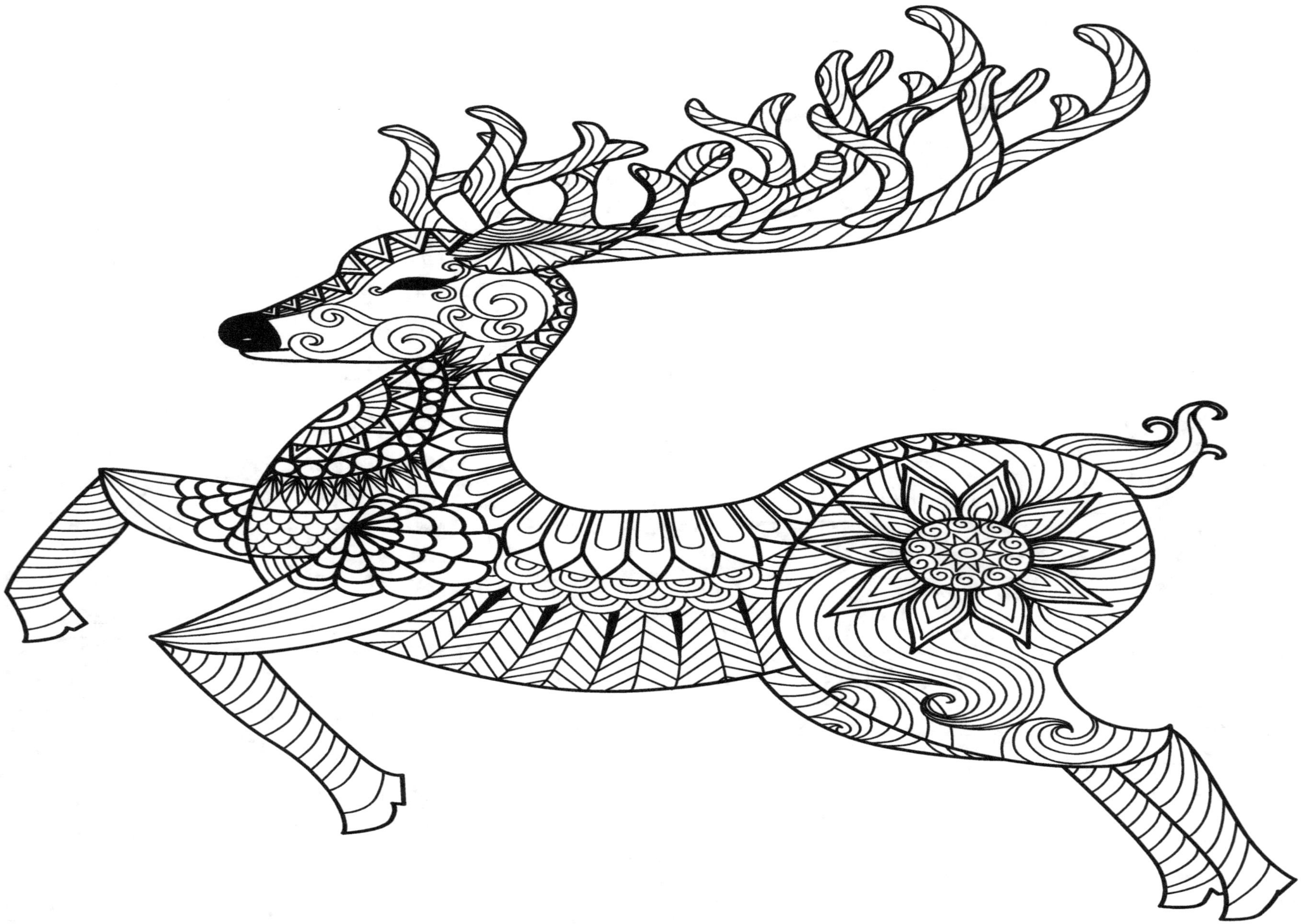

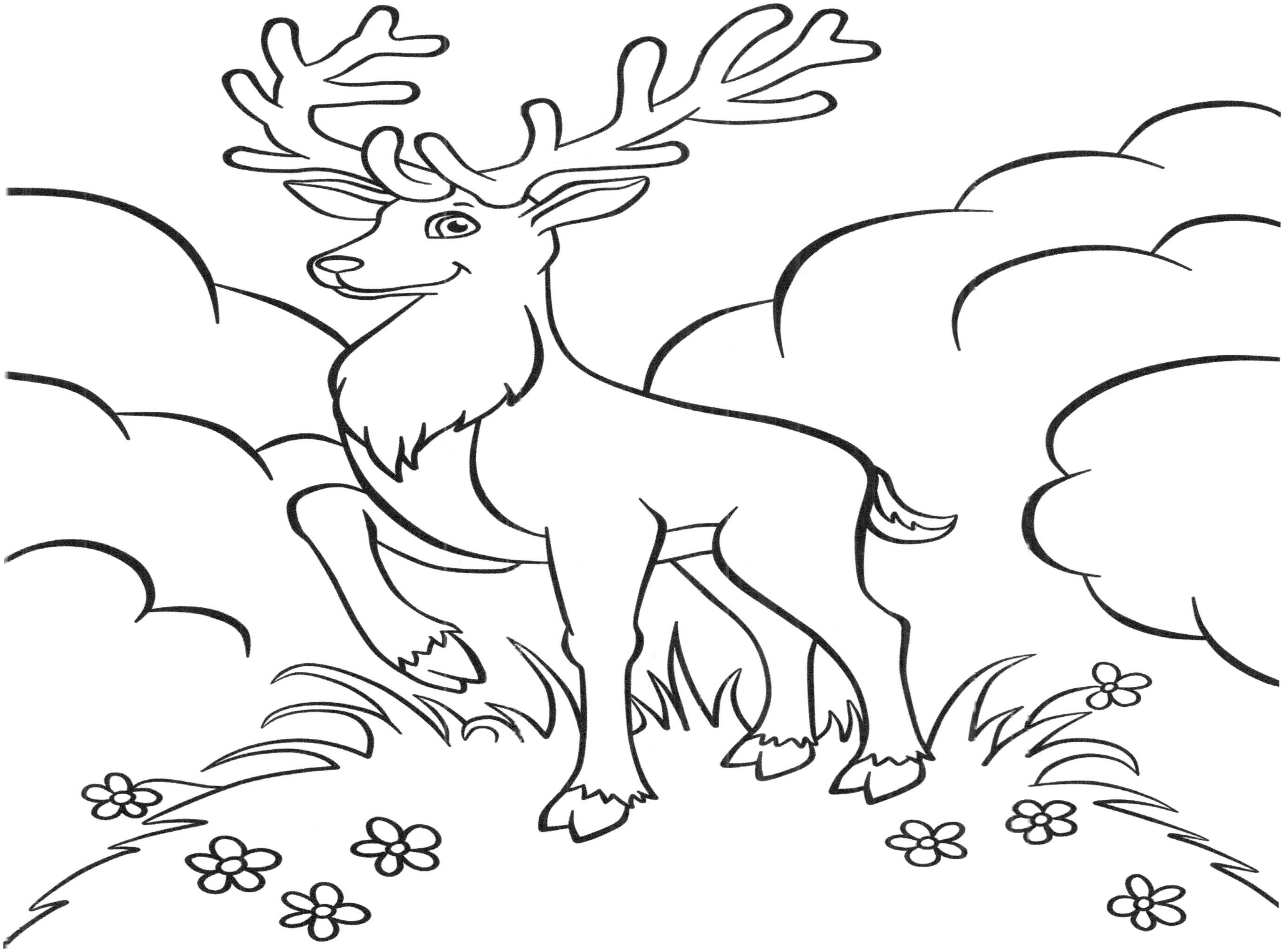

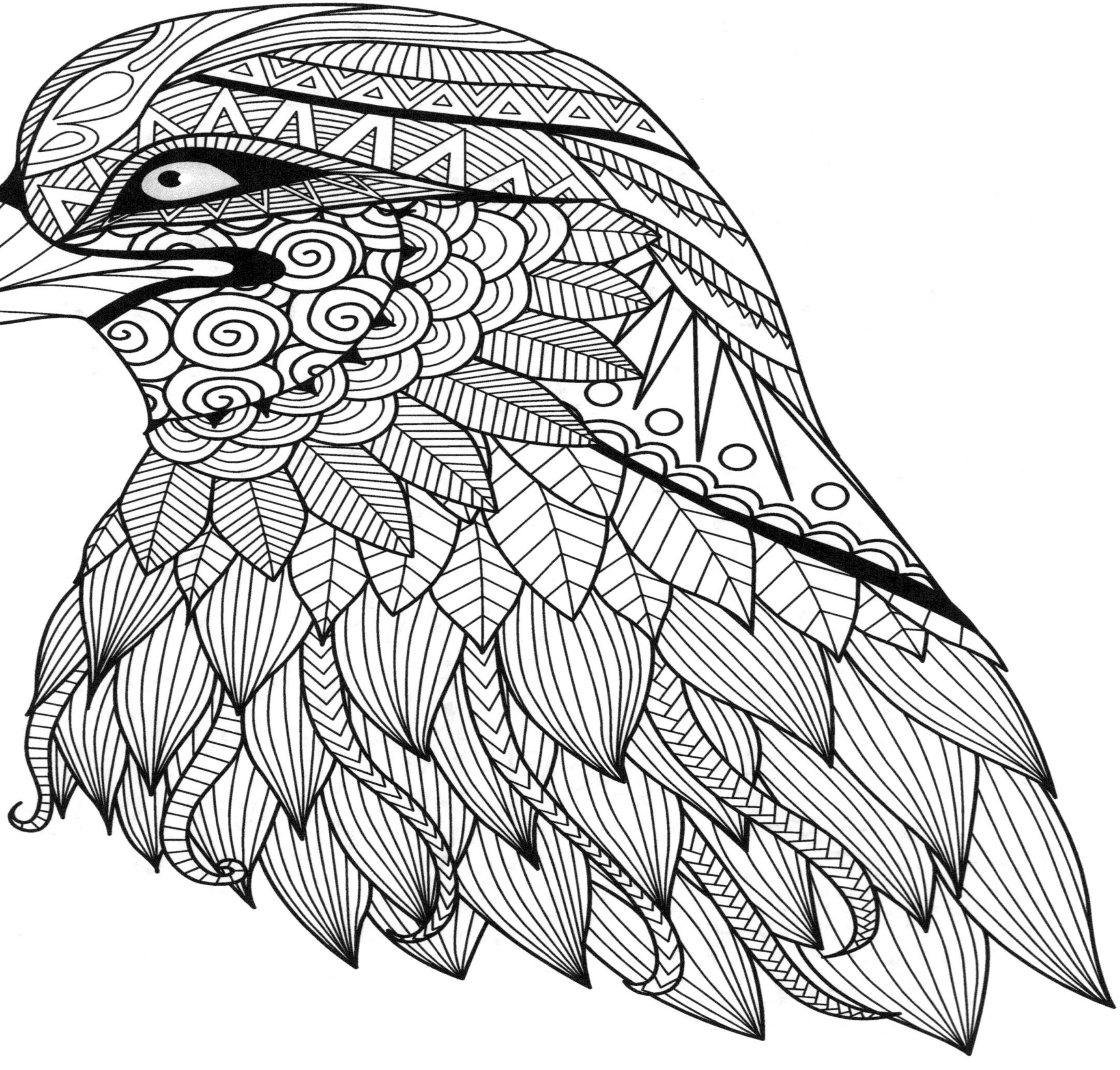

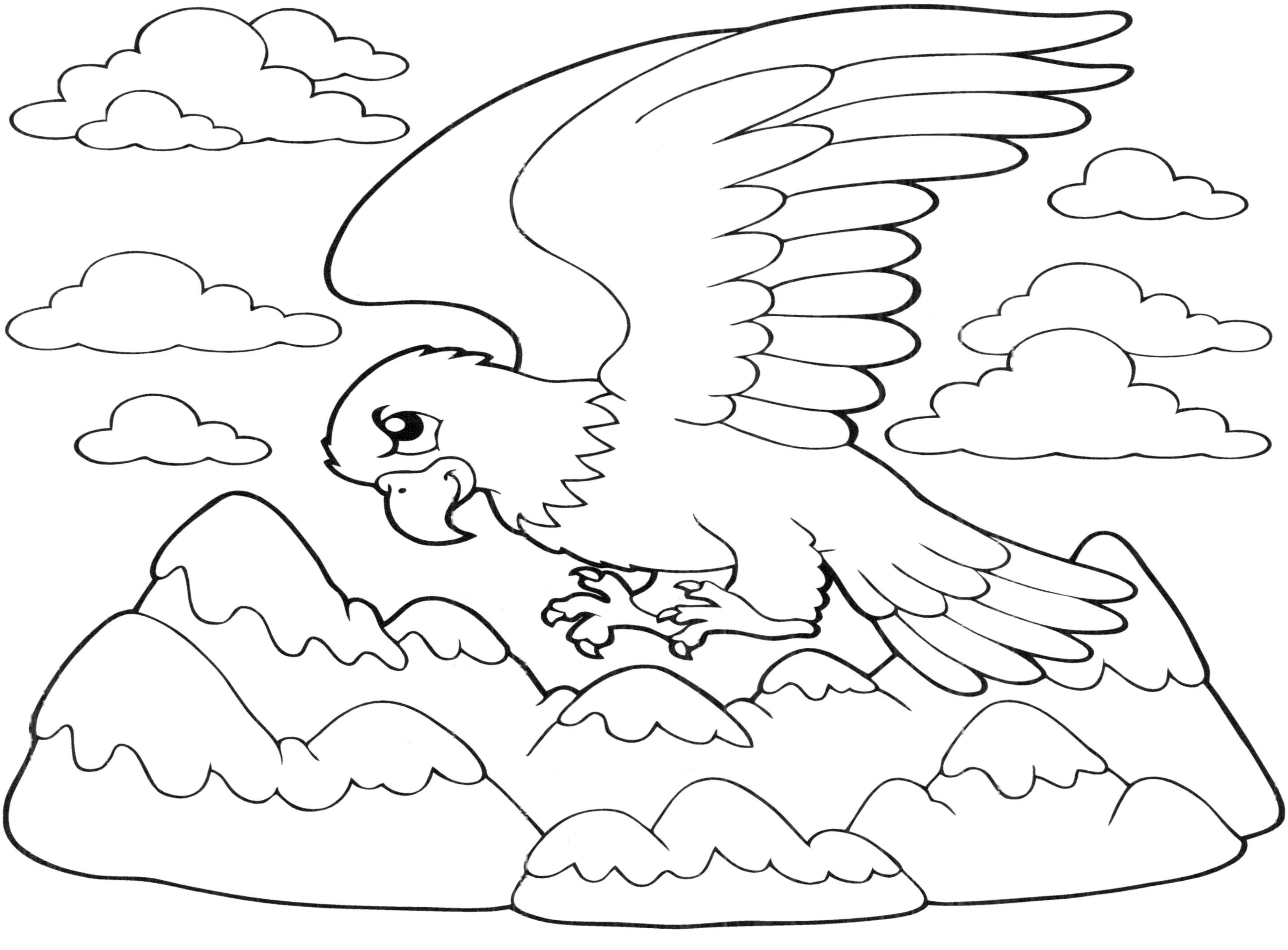

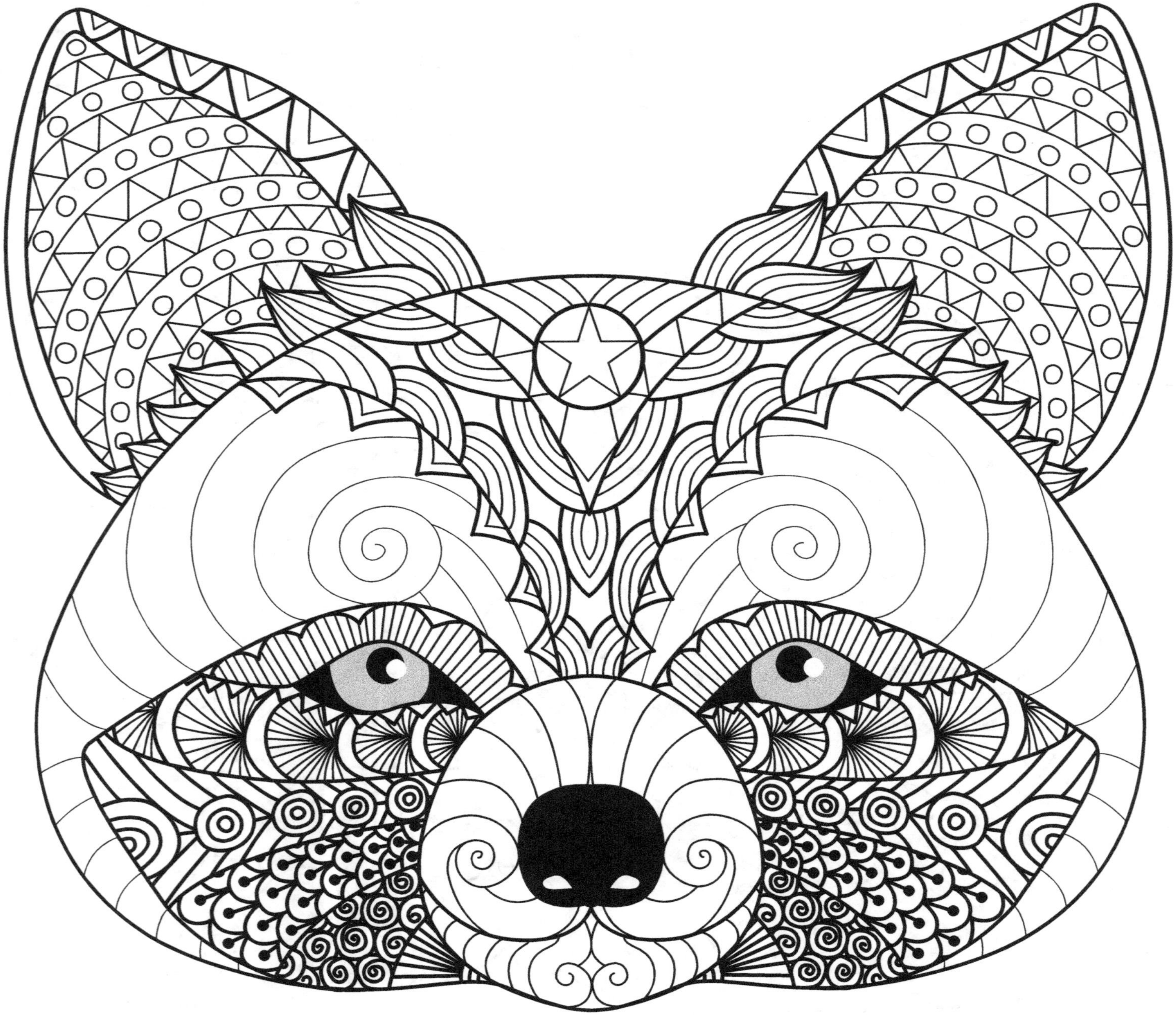

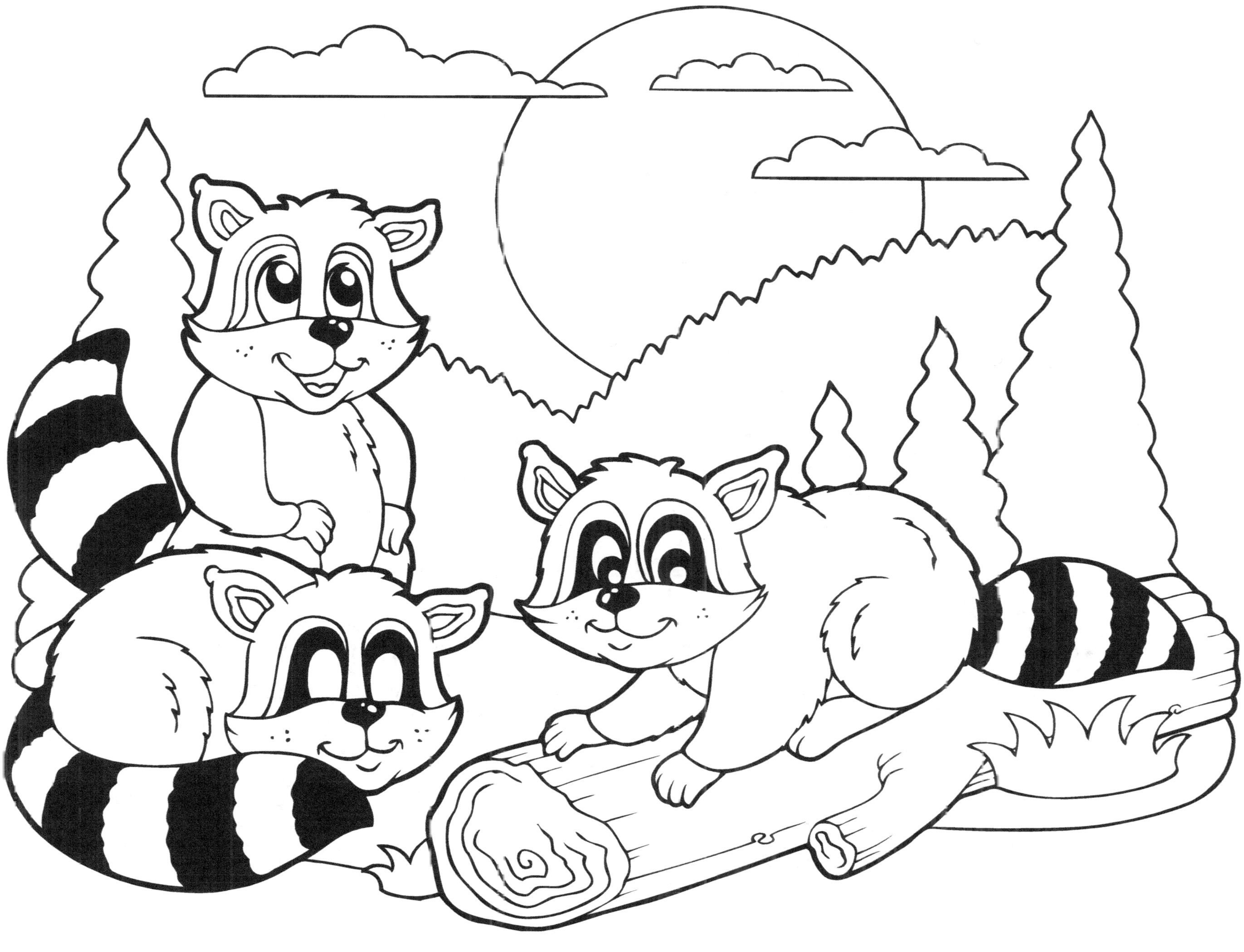

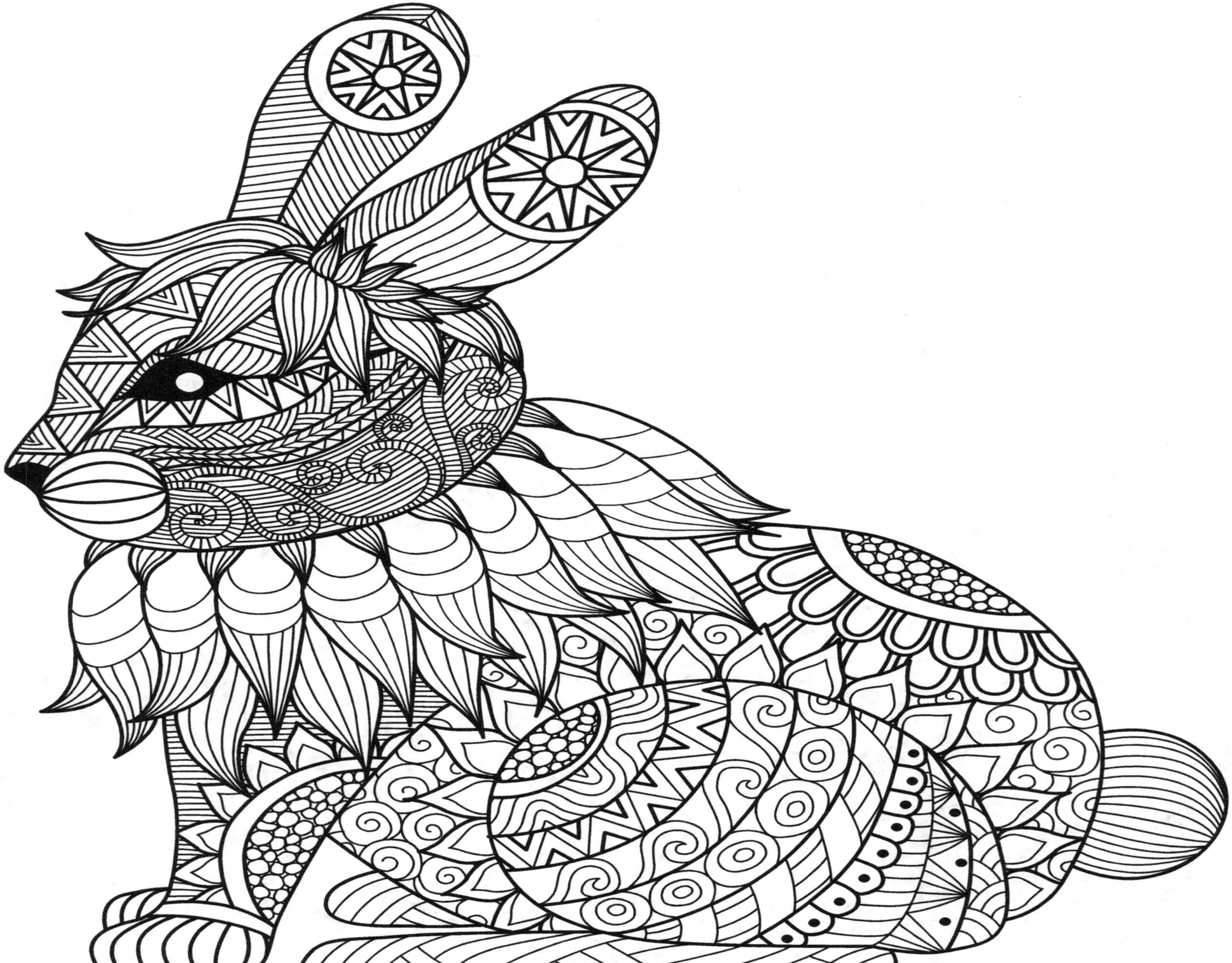

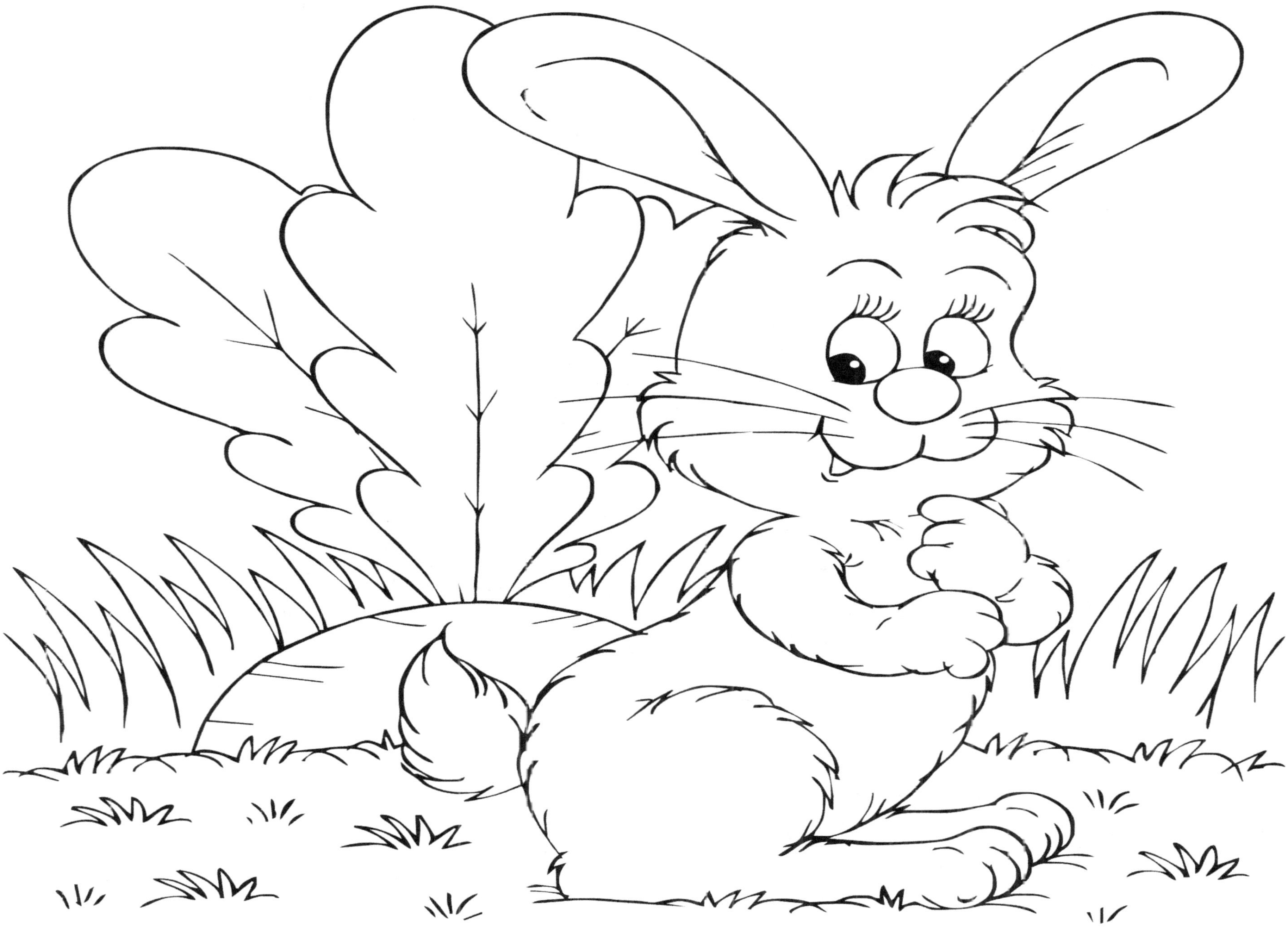

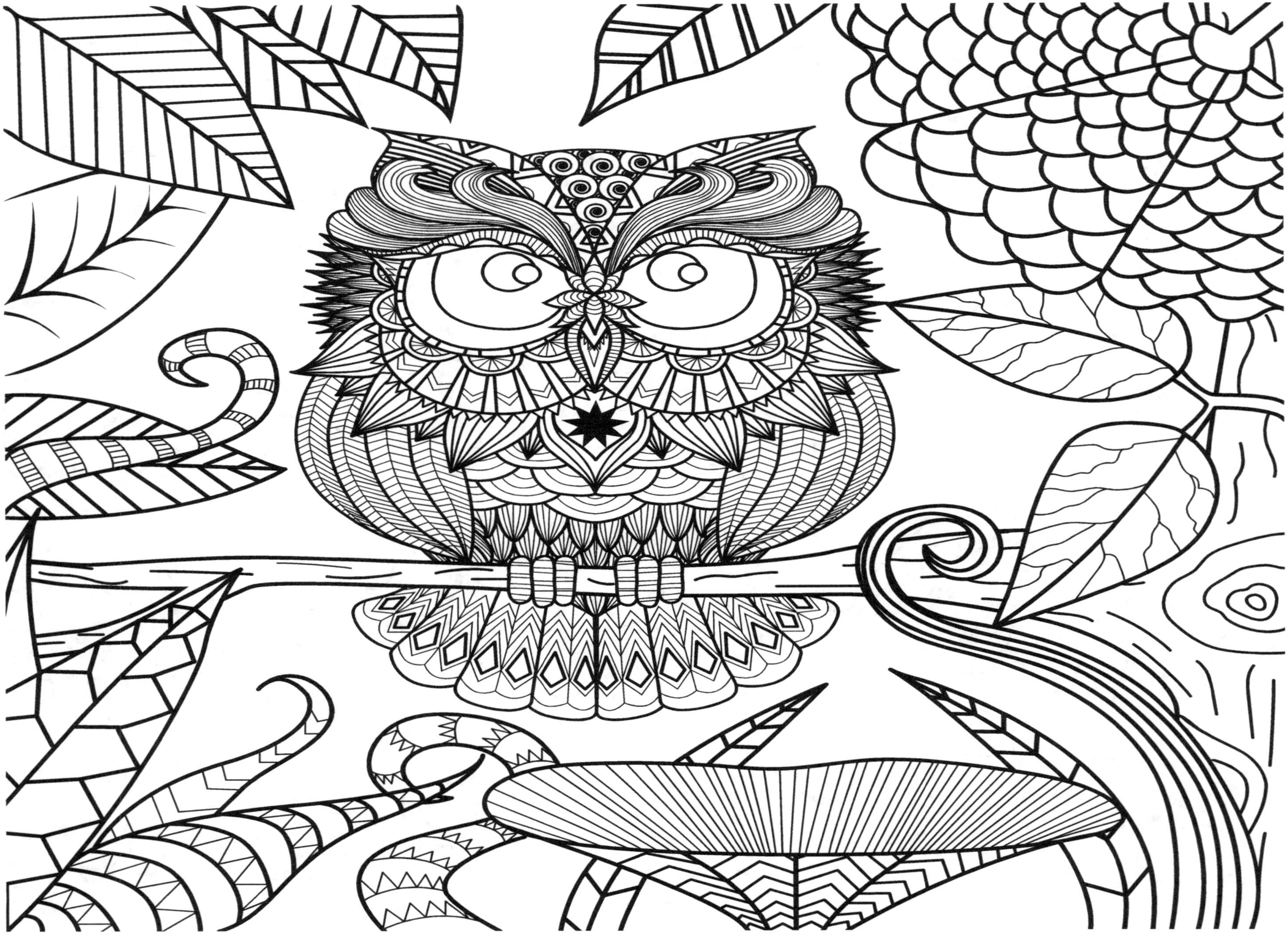

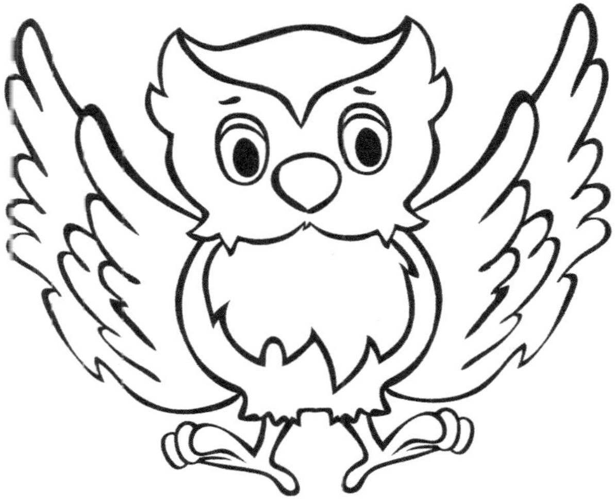
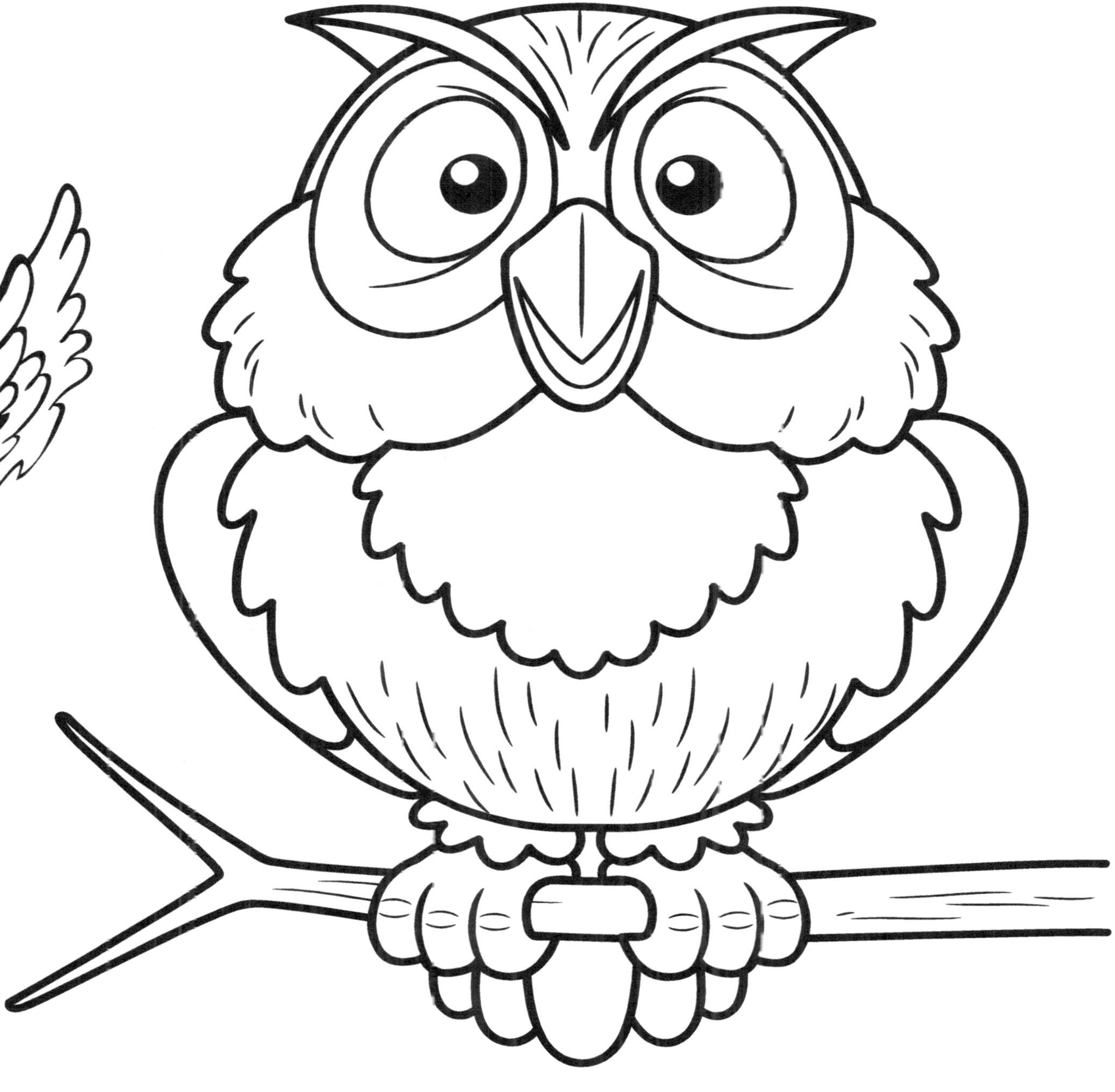

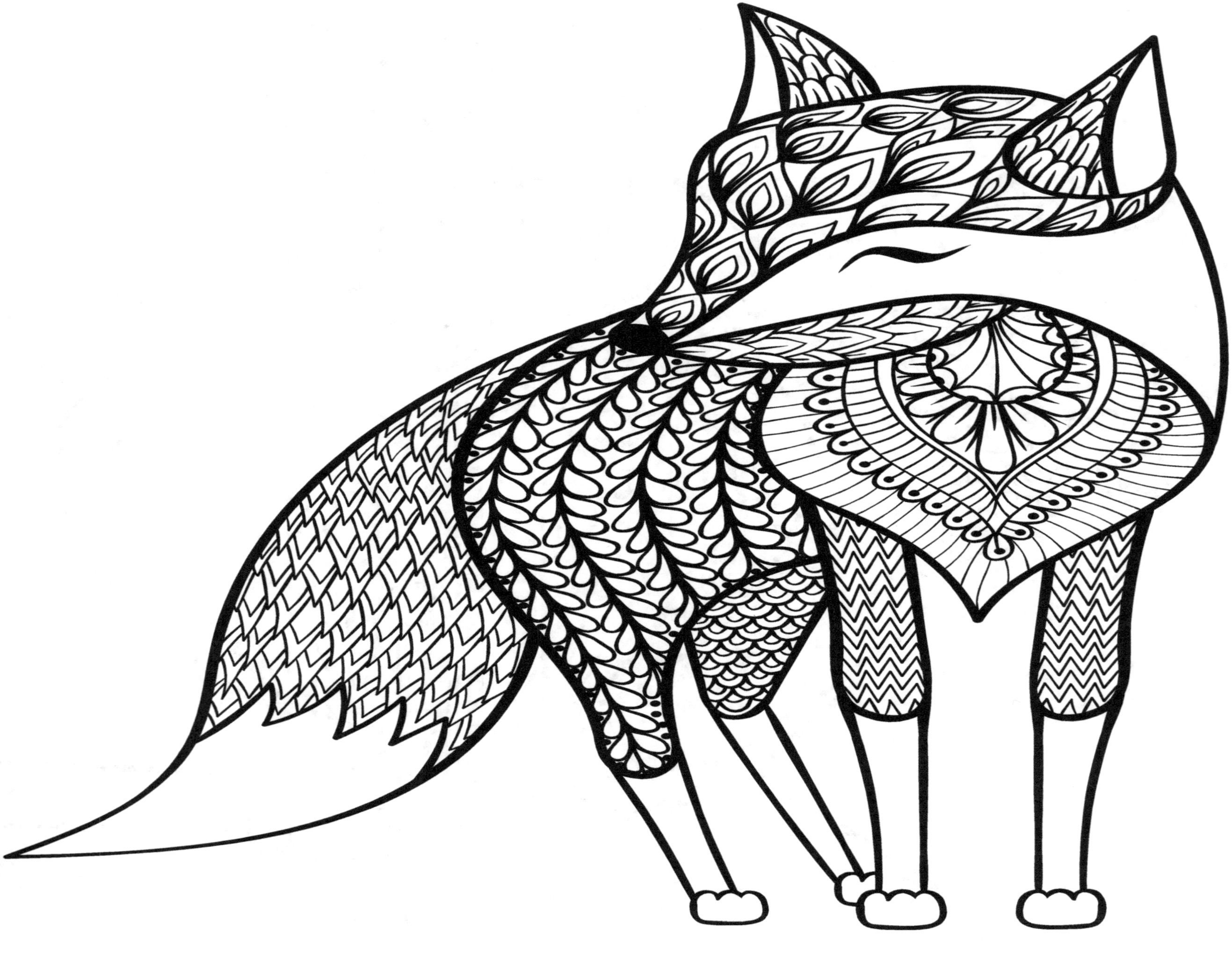

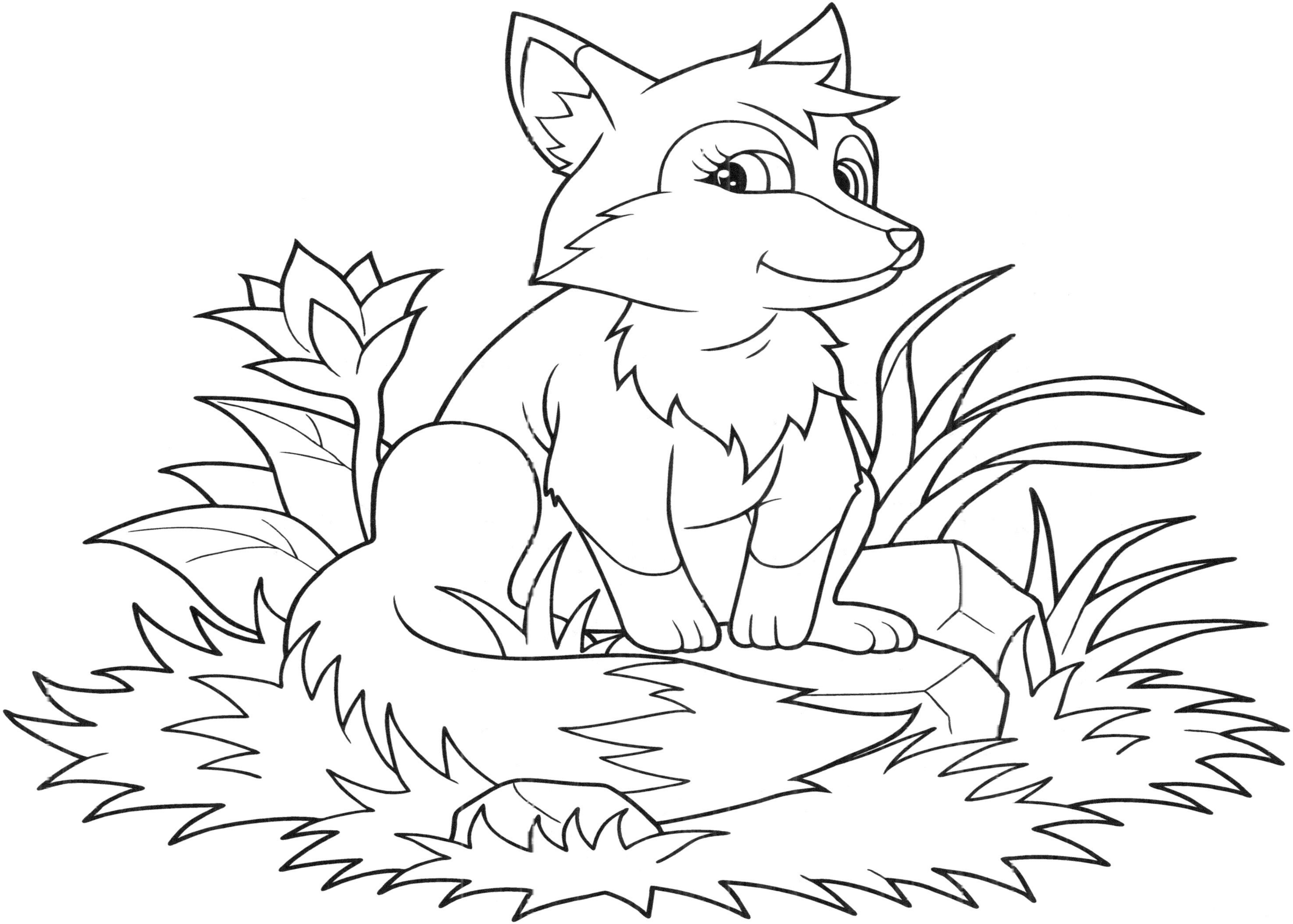

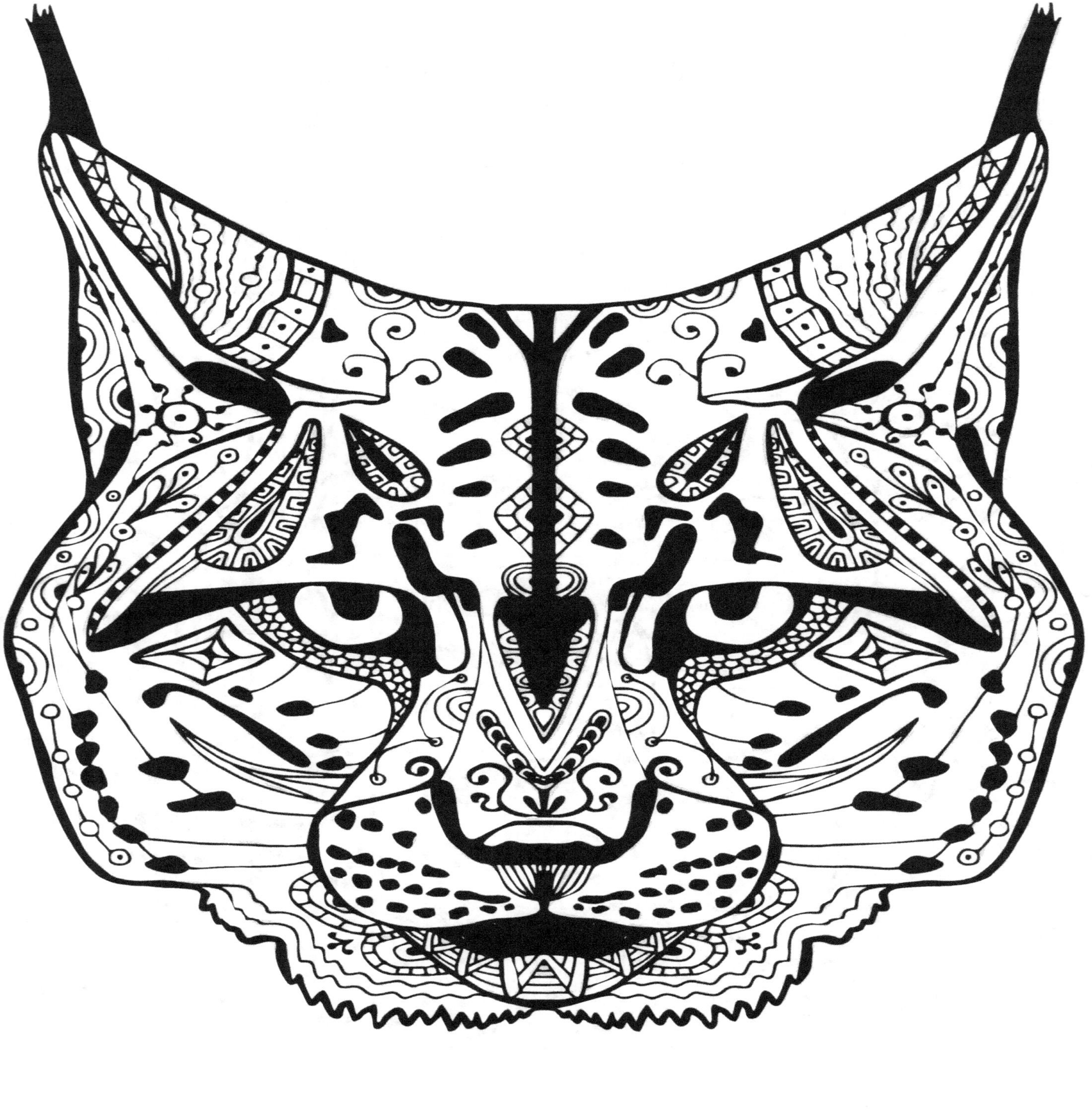

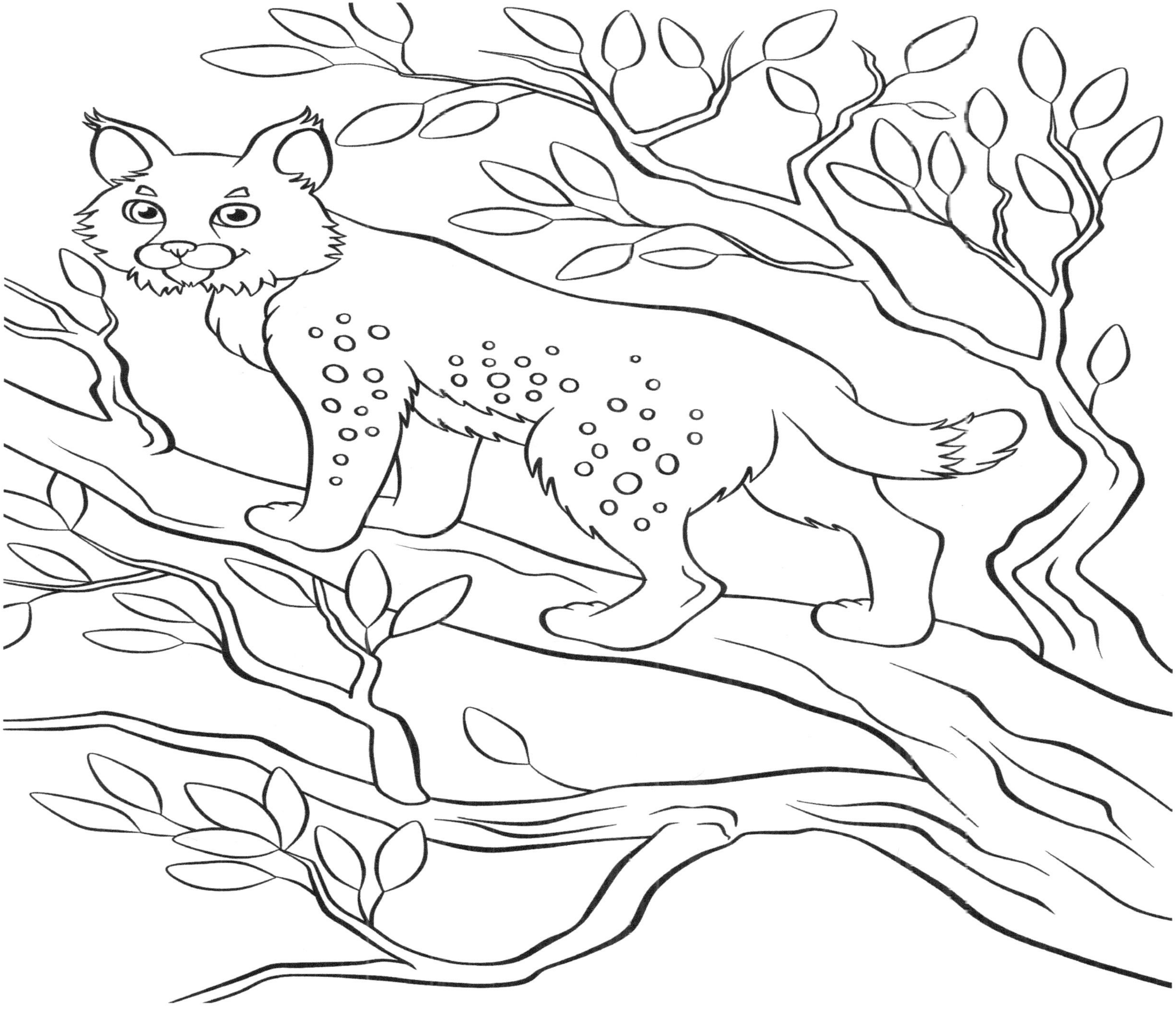

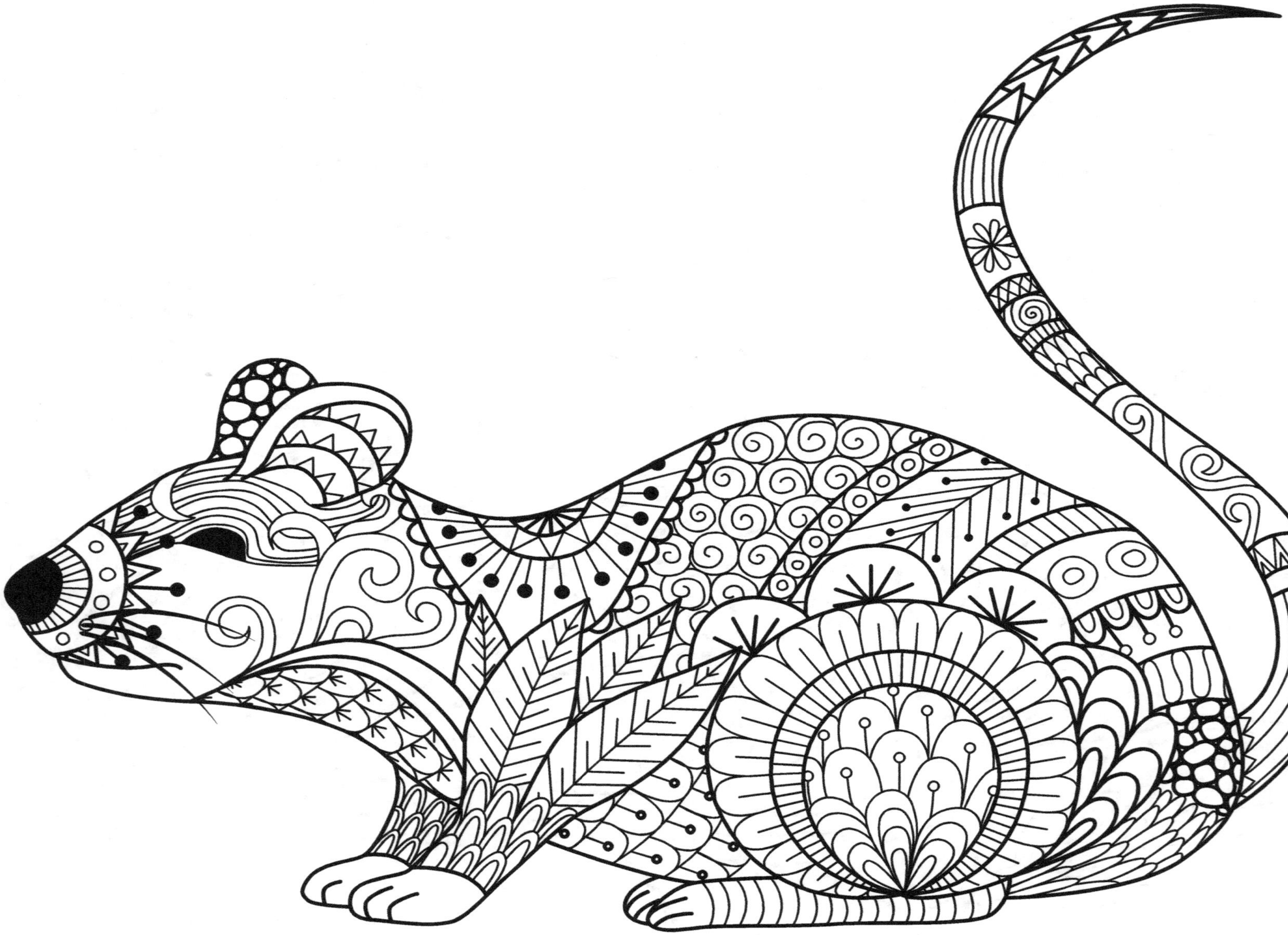

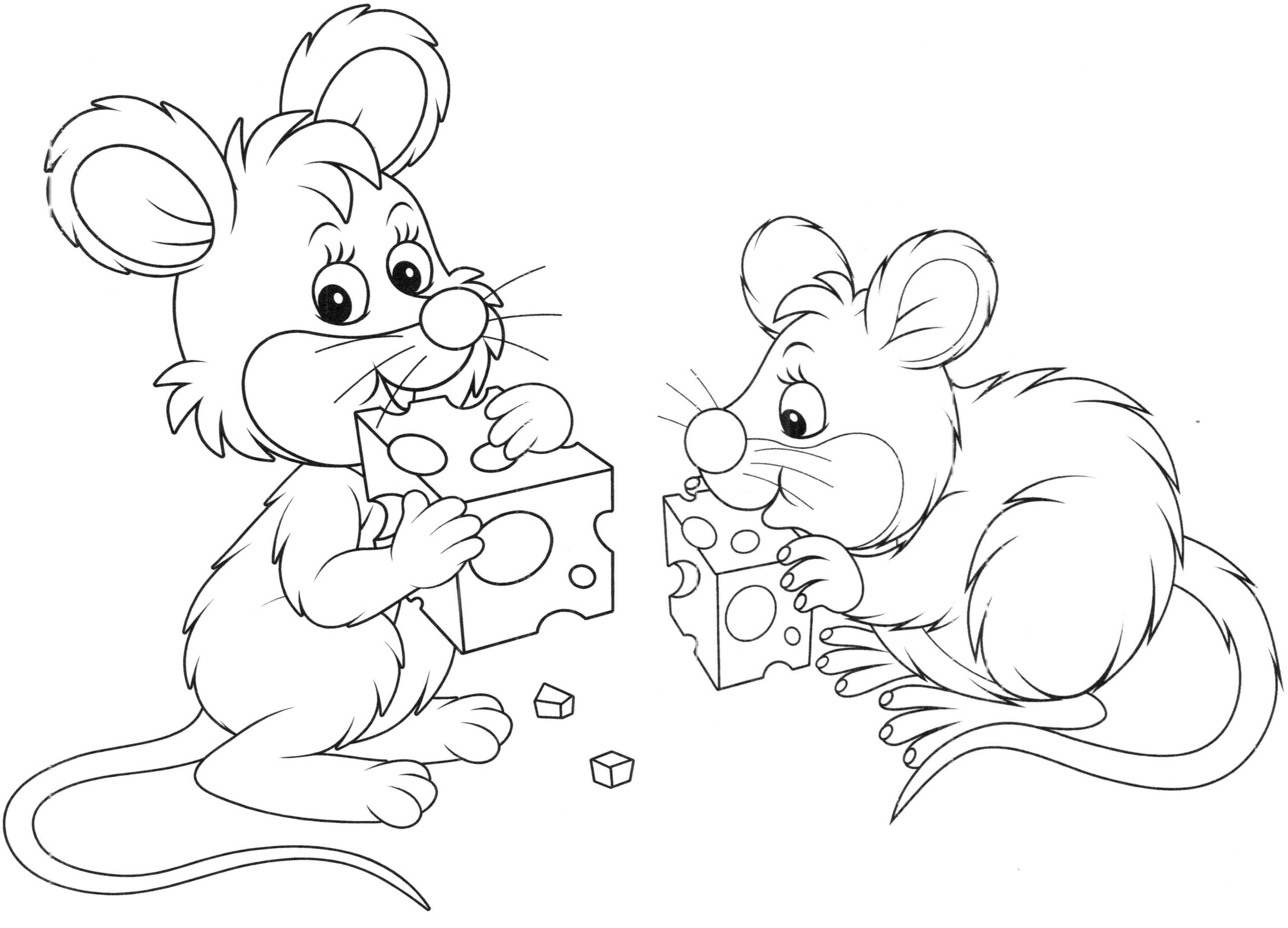

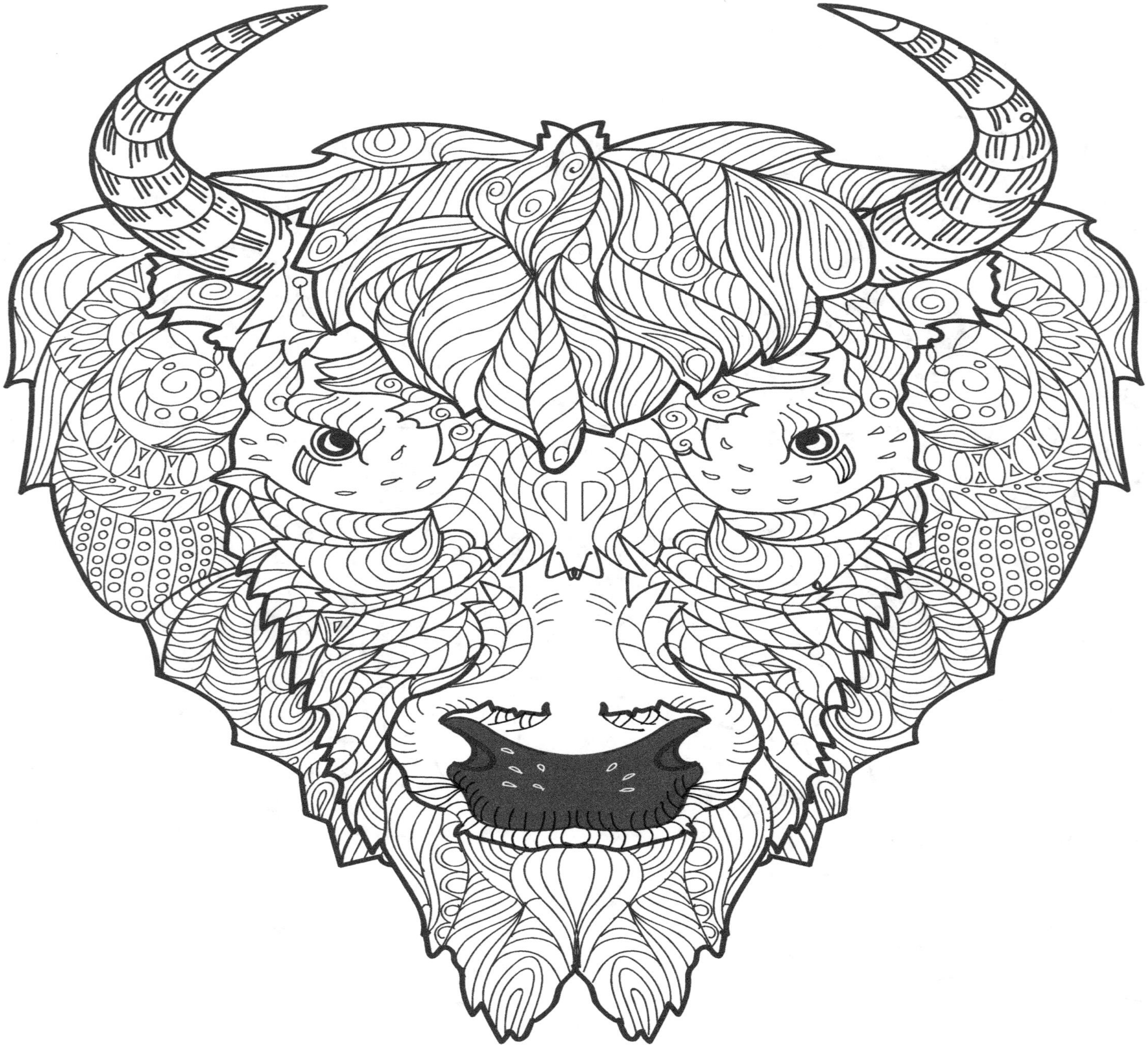

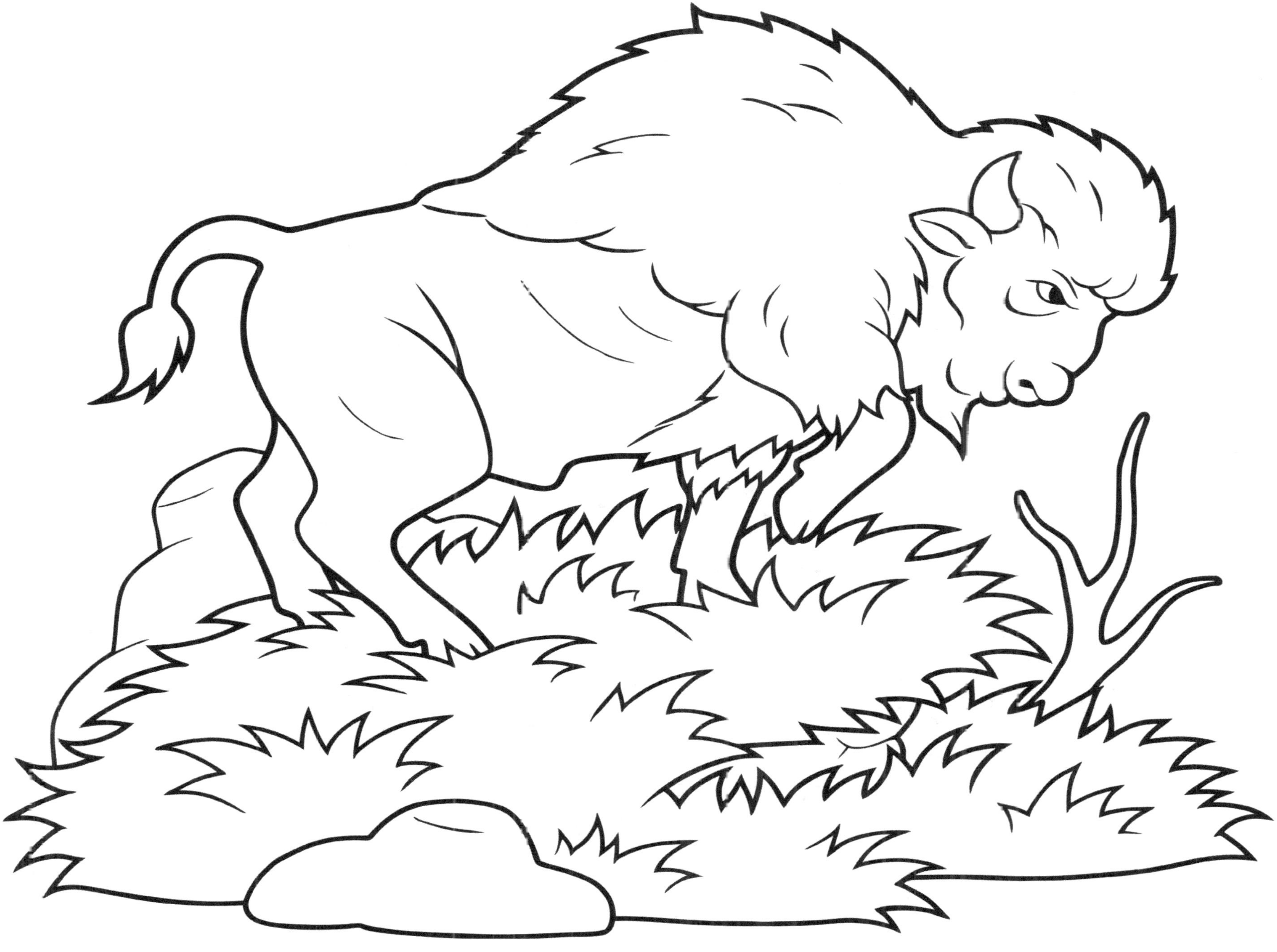

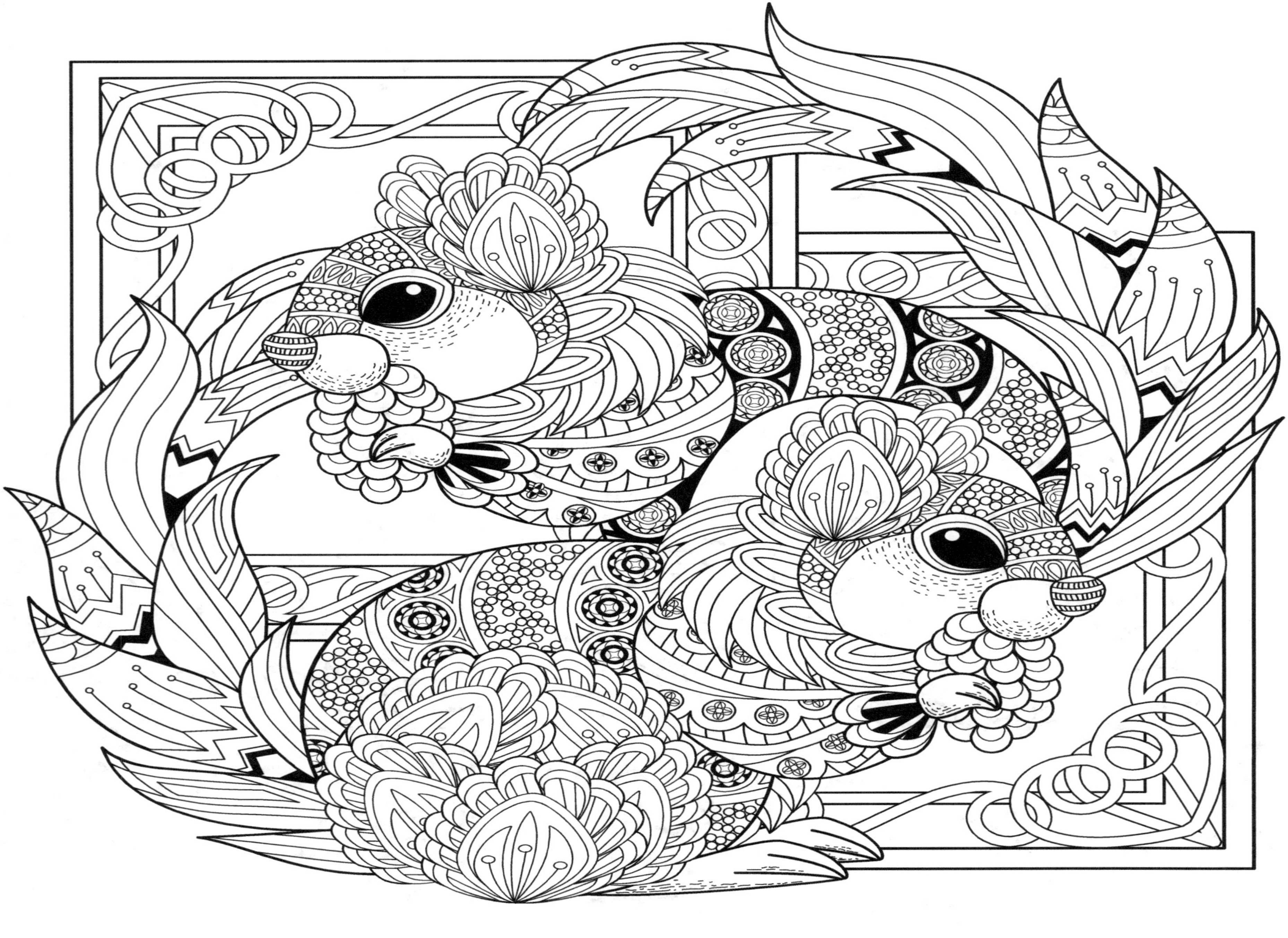

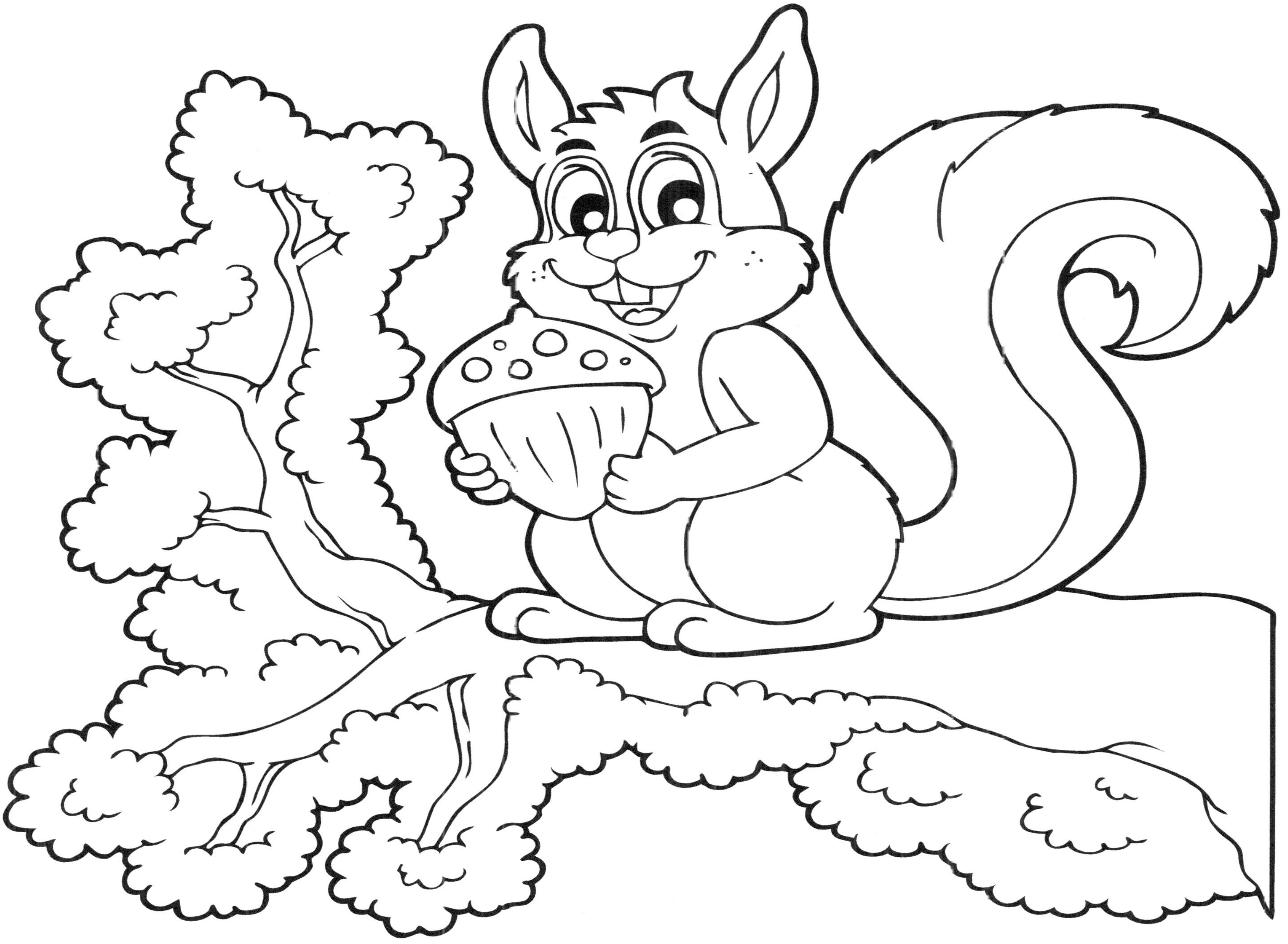

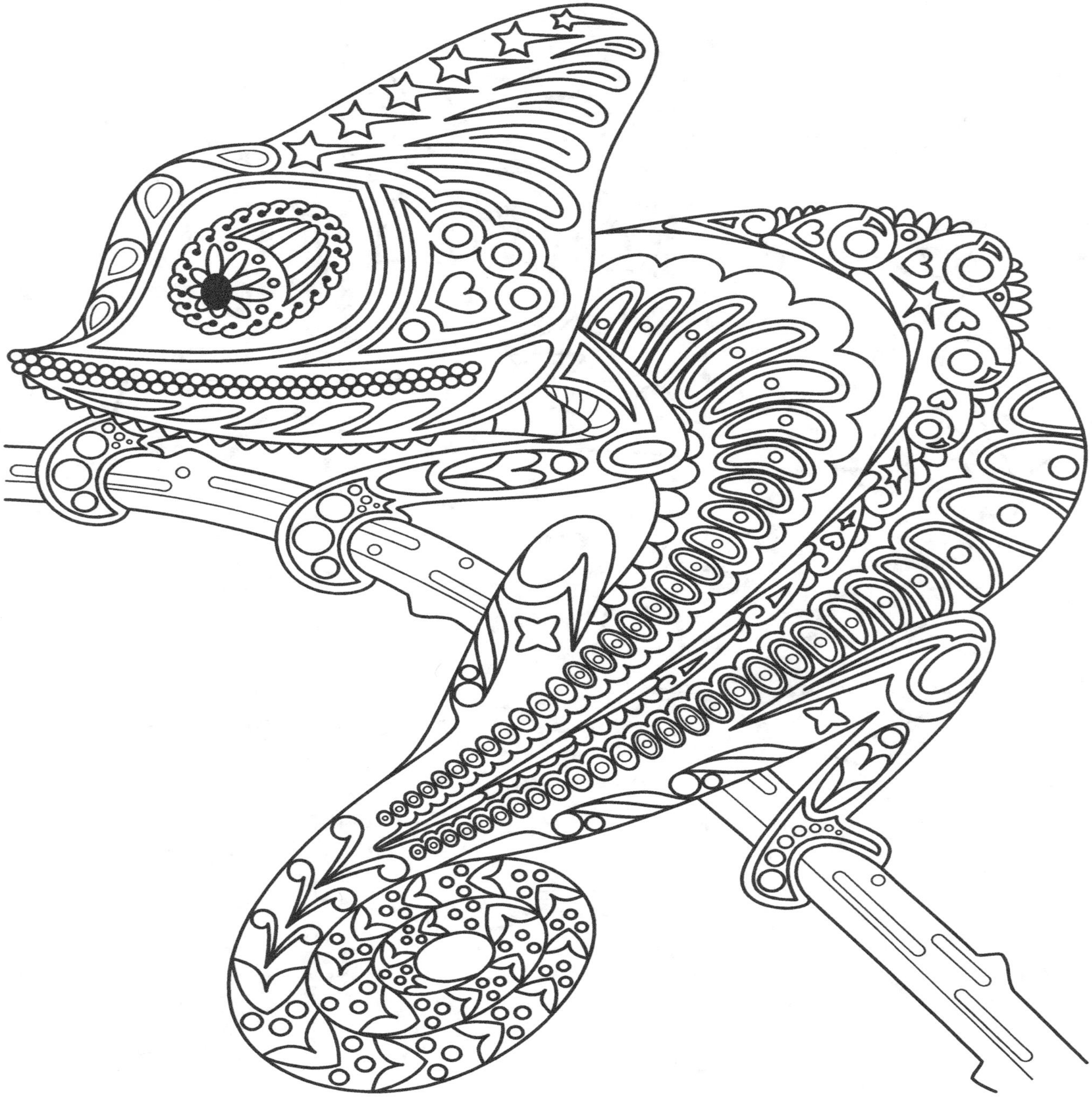

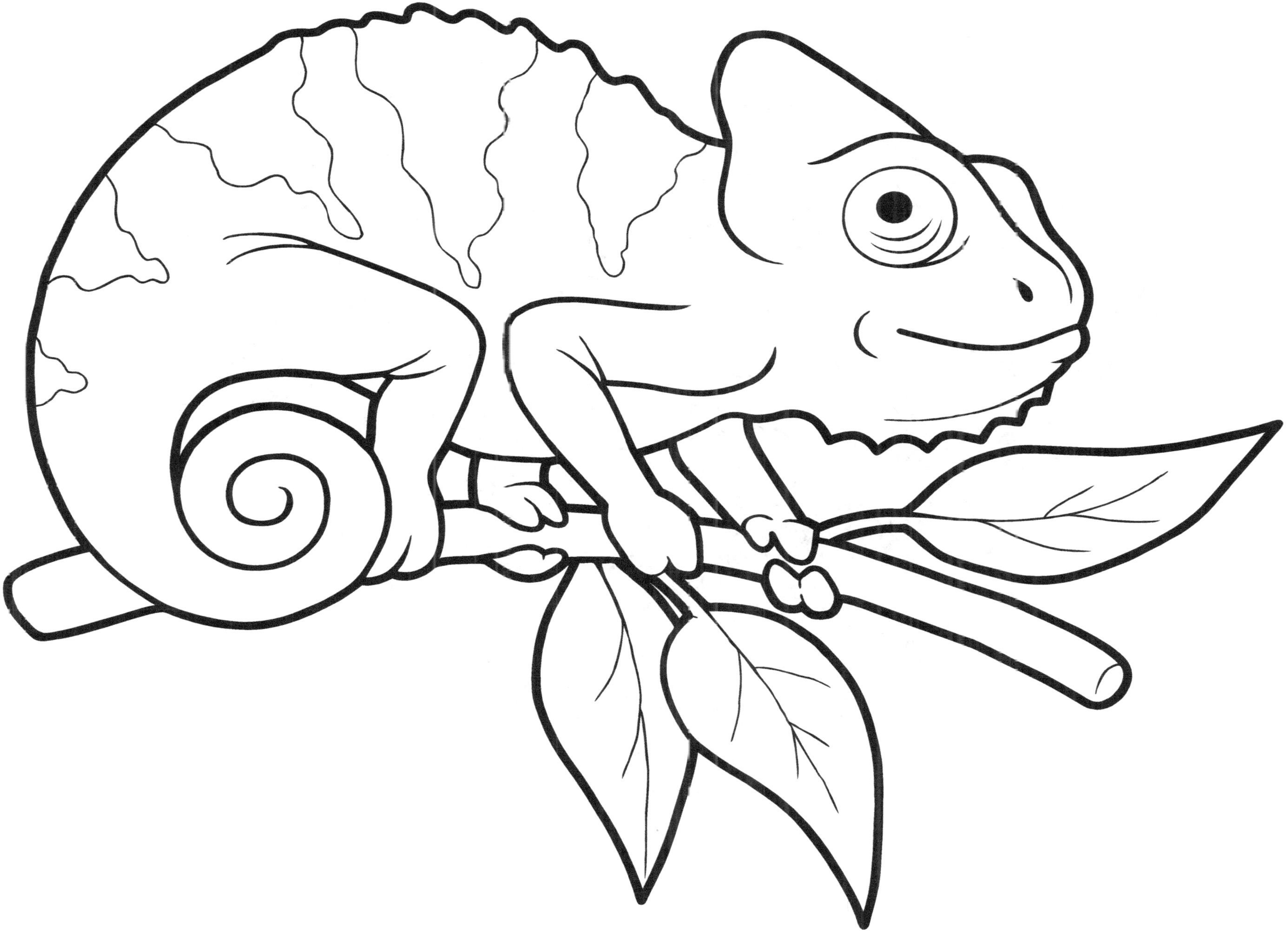

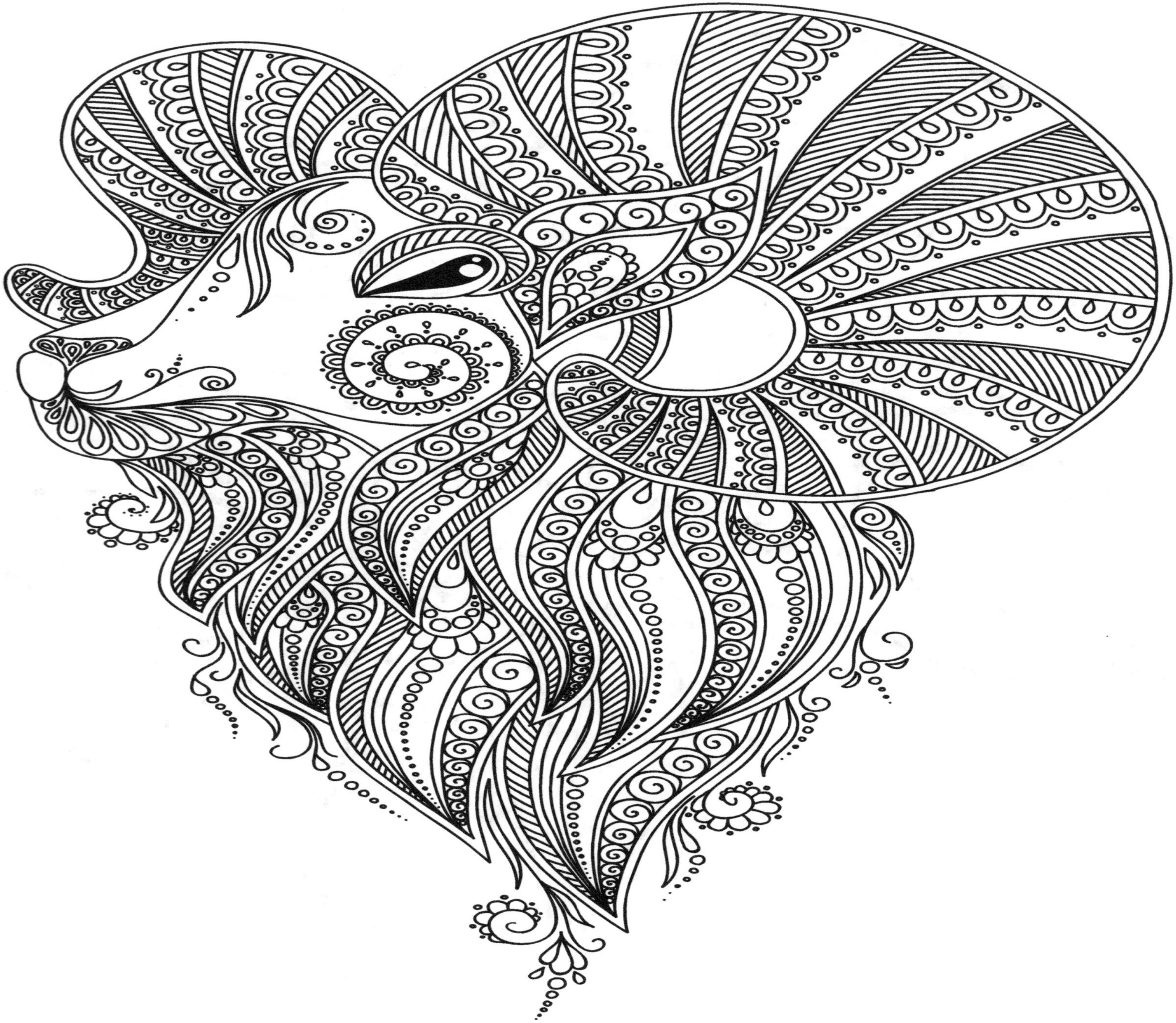

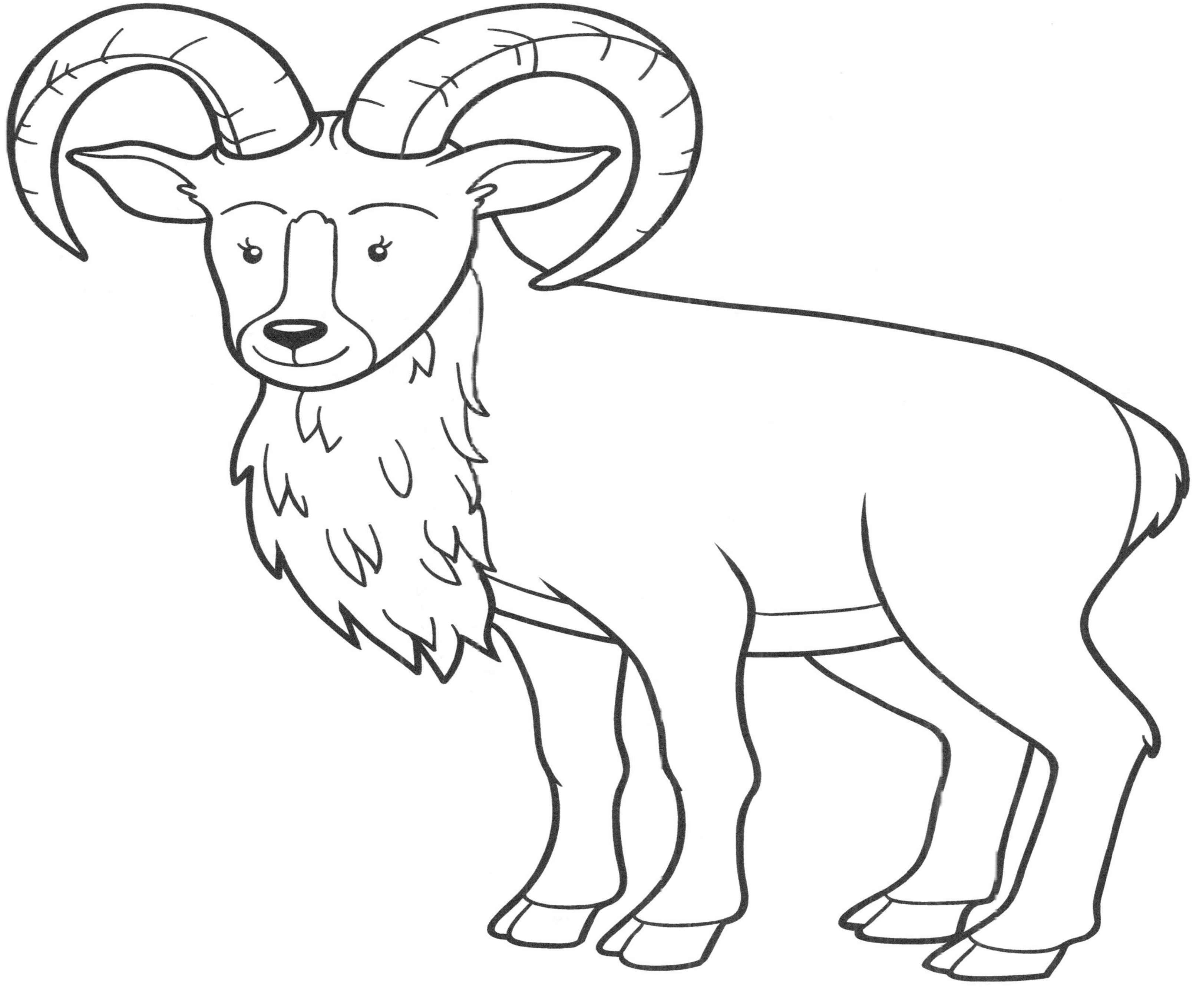

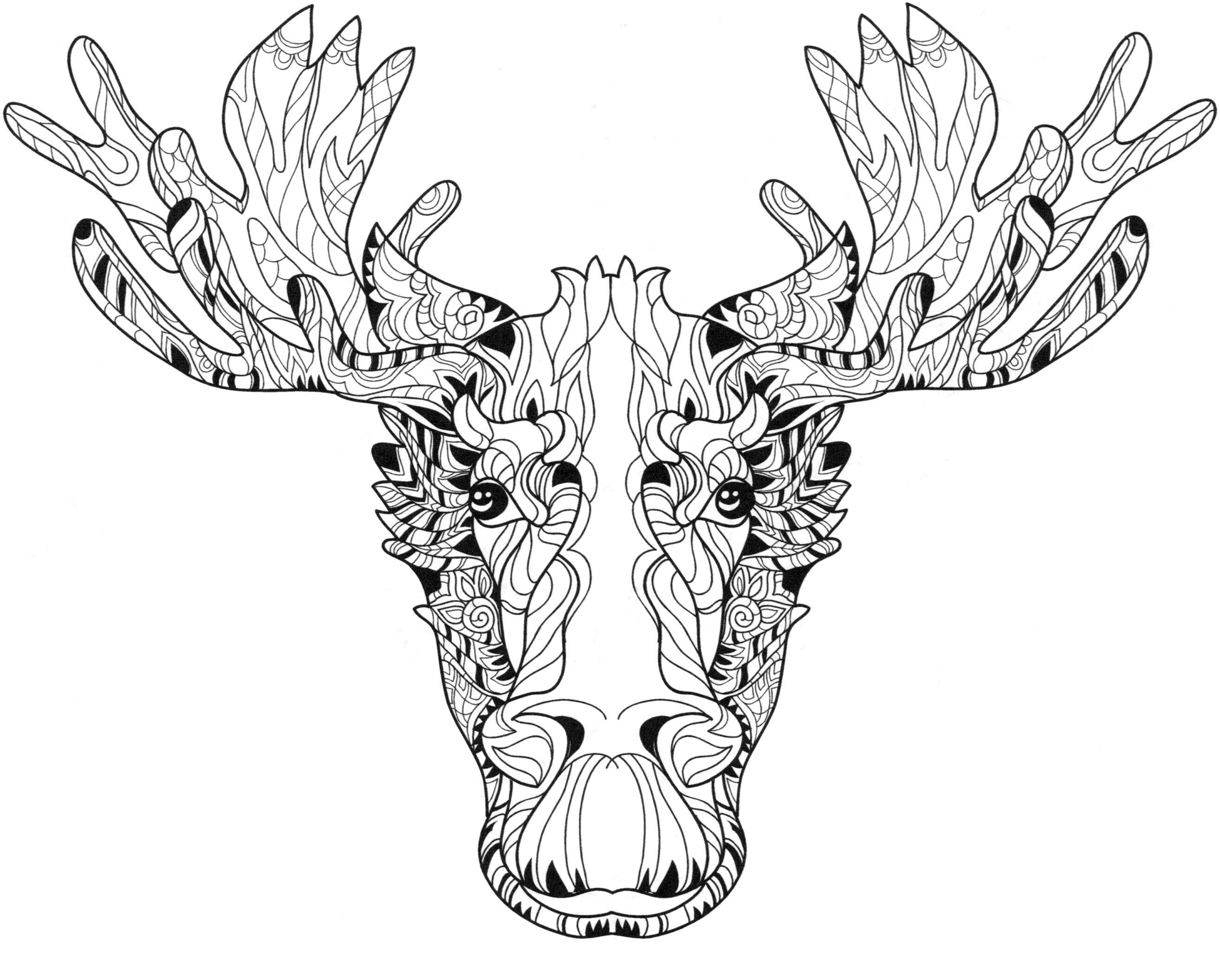

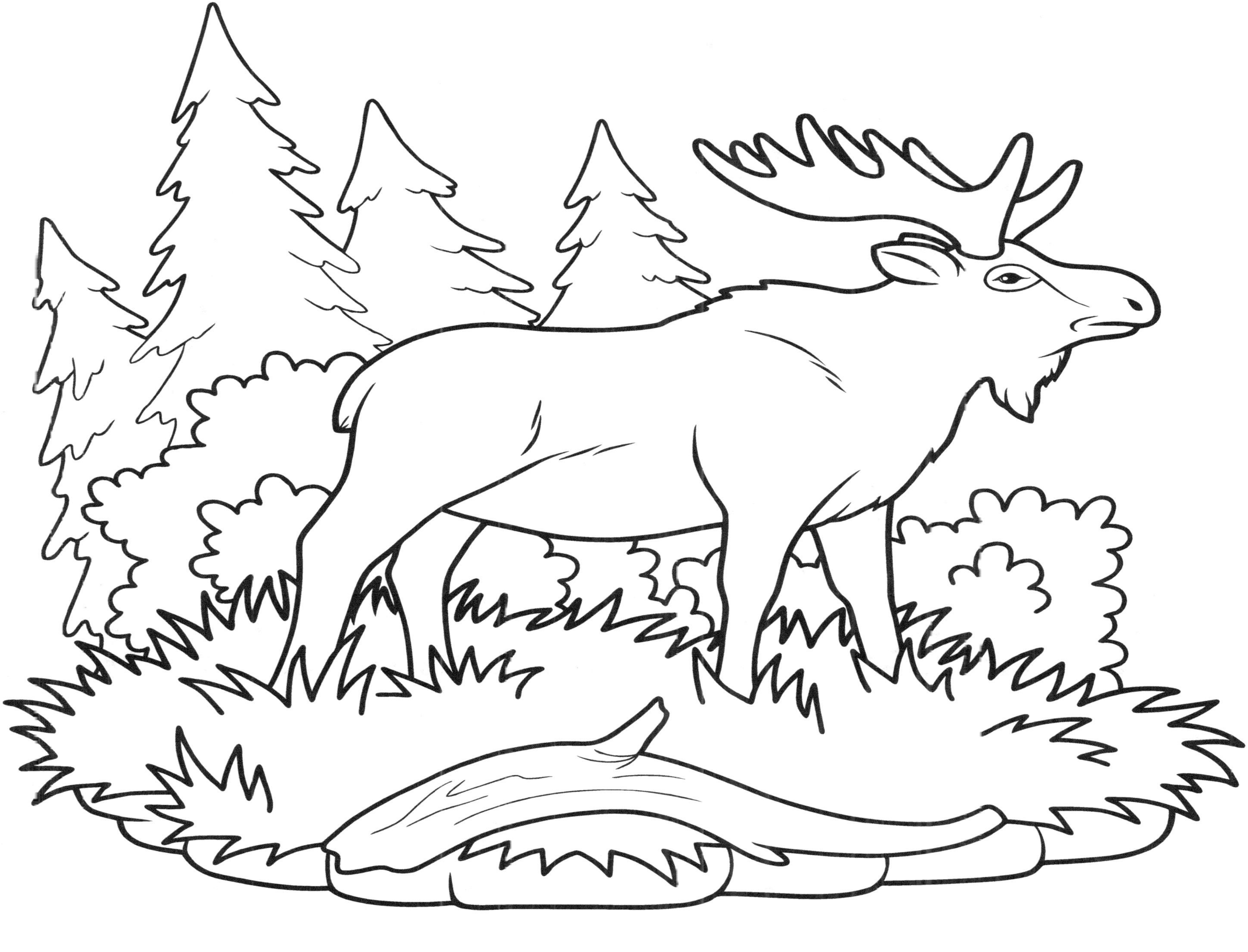

Adventure Learning Press
adventurelearningpress.com
adventurelearningpress@gmail.com